KU-175-388

AS

VISUAL
REVISION
GUIDE

SUCCESS

BUSINESS STUDIES

David Floyd

Contents

External influences

Objectives and strategy

Marketing

Finance and accounting

People in organisations

Operations management

Market forces

Business cycle

- All economies are affected by business (trade) cycles. These cycles show whether overall (aggregate) demand is rising or falling. (A recession is when there is a downturn in aggregate demand. A recovery is when demand starts to grow again.)

- The nature of the product often determines the extent to which it is affected by changes in the business cycle. For example, when there is a recession, the demand for luxury products is normally affected more than the demand for necessities.

- Some businesses may survive home-based economic downturns by trading in overseas markets that are less affected by recession.

Stage	Firms
Recession: contracting output; gloomy outlook	experience falling demand and so cut prices and dismiss staff; losses are made; investment falls; some go out of business.
Recovery: the economy starts expanding; rising, but limited, expectations	experience increase in demand; review their employment and investment positions but still lack confidence.
Boom: rapid growth in output; high confidence but fear of inflation	invest and take on staff; may find skill shortages; increase prices and profit margins; utilise spare capacity.
Downturn: growth slows again	experience falling demand and profits; start reducing output and investment.

Competition

- The level of competition influences demand, e.g. in terms of the number of substitutes available, and the amount of marketing and other resources devoted to the product. The two (often theoretical) extreme market situations are:
  1 a **perfectly competitive** market – this contains many firms that are **price-takers** (no one firm can set prices that other firms follow), and there is free entry and exit of these firms to keep competition at its highest
  2 a **monopoly** market – this consists of a single seller who can therefore **set prices** because there are no product substitutes and no competition.

- Many products are traded in an **oligopolistic** market, where there are few suppliers, who may differentiate their products through the use of branding and marketing techniques. In practice, barriers to entry may exist through small-scale competitors not being able to compete as a result of not benefiting from economies of scale.

- A market operating under **monopolistic competition** conditions has many more sellers, with greater freedom to enter and leave the market, and price-taking rather than the price-making often found with oligopolies.

- These different forms of market competition exist in the various sectors of the UK economy. One popular classification is:
  primary – extractive industries, e.g. fishing, farming and forestry
  secondary – manufacturing and construction firms
  tertiary – service suppliers, e.g. banks, transport, retailers.

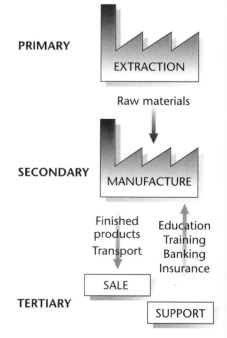

PRIMARY — EXTRACTION

Raw materials

SECONDARY — MANUFACTURE

Finished products Transport

Education Training Banking Insurance

SALE

TERTIARY

SUPPORT

Demand and supply

The demand for, and supply of, products are the major market forces in a competitive market. In such a market, businesses seek to make profits, and prices are controlled through the interaction of **demand** and **supply** (i.e. the interaction of buyers and sellers).

This graph shows that 30 000 items are demanded when the price is £10. If the price falls to £5, quantity demanded increases to 40 000

This shows that, at a price of £10, firms are prepared to supply 30 000 items

The **equilibrium price** is where demand equals supply

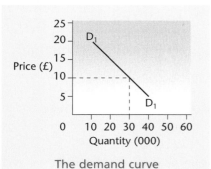

The demand curve

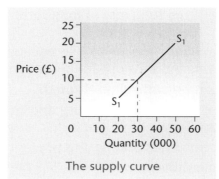

The supply curve

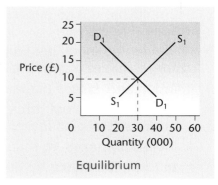

Equilibrium

Prices can move freely. In the above situation if the price rose to £15:

- consumers demand 20 000 but producers supply 40 000
- this surplus causes producers to reduce the price
- the lower price increases quantity demanded but reduces quantity supplied
- equilibrium is re-established.

- Where **profits** exist in a market, new firms may be encouraged to enter.
- Increased competition should lead to the least efficient firms leaving the market, as their profit levels fall (or turn into losses).
- The consumer is the decision-maker, the results of consumers' buying decisions affecting whether firms stay in the market or leave it.
- The entry and exit of firms into a market, and the expansion and contraction of existing firms in the market, ensure resources – land, labour, capital and enterprise – are reallocated between these firms, and that they are used efficiently.
- In practice, the demand for a product is influenced by many factors. These include the level of income, the degree of competition, and changes in society (e.g. fashion and taste, laws) and technology.

EXAMINER'S TOP TIP
Learn how to construct demand and supply diagrams to illustrate different business situations and examples.

Quick test

1 **Distinguish between a recession and a recovery.**

2 **Give one example of a good and of a service that would normally be classified as luxury goods.**

3 **Give two examples of substitutes commonly found in a supermarket.**

4 **Give one example of an oligopolistic market and of a market where monopolistic competition exists.**

5 **Name the three sectors of the UK economy.**

6 **Give an example of a business in each of the three sectors of the UK economy.**

7 **Give one example of a market where demand often exceeds supply and one where supply often exceeds demand.**

1. recession: a downturn in aggregate demand; recovery: demand starts to grow again 2. good: e.g. jewellery, sports car, yacht; hi-fi system; service: e.g. holidays, private health insurance, personal trainer, manicure 3. meats, e.g. ham and chicken; spreads, e.g. butter and margarine 4. oligopoly: certain foodstuffs and household items, e.g. washing powders/liquids; monopolistic competition: e.g. double-glazing, hairdressing, plumbing 5. primary, secondary, tertiary 6. primary: e.g. a local farm, a fishing fleet; secondary: e.g. a car-manufacturer, a local builder; tertiary: e.g. a supermarket, an insurance company 7. demand exceeding supply: e.g. concert tickets for popular entertainers or major sporting events; supply exceeds demand: e.g. anything that has gone out of fashion, such as clothes, computer games, furniture

Interest and exchange rates

The need to control inflation

- The UK government has the control of inflation as one of its key economic objectives.
- Interest rates and fiscal policy are key measures used to control inflation and the level of demand.
- Increasing demand can encourage supply and economic growth, lead to a fall in unemployment, and encourage firms to invest in long-term growth by investing in capital items.
- However, too much demand can cause prices to rise because supply (of skilled labour and other resources) cannot meet this increased level of demand.
- Inflation and excess demand can be controlled through:
  - increasing interest rates, to discourage borrowing and therefore spending; however, business will also invest less
  - increasing taxes, to reduce consumer purchasing power
  - reducing spending by the government.

Interest rates

- The government's monetary policy is carried out by the Bank of England's Monetary Policy Committee (MPC) which determines, independently of the government, the level of interest rates in order to help control inflation.
- Higher interest rates discourage borrowing by individuals and firms, and increase the cost of existing borrowing (e.g. mortgages); as a result, less money is available to spend, and there is less incentive to borrow.
- The risk of using interest rates to control inflation is that the cut in borrowing that results will move the economy into a recession.
- Changing interest rates also have an effect on exchange rates:

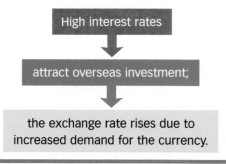
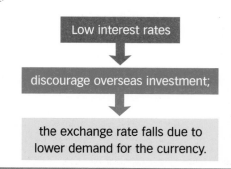

Fiscal policy

- Taxes reduce purchasing power because they reduce personal and company incomes, so raising taxes takes spending power out of the economy.
- The government may alter the rates of <u>direct taxes</u>: these are taxes (Income Tax and National Insurance) set as a percentage of <u>incomes</u>.
- <u>Indirect taxes</u> are based on people's <u>spending</u>: <u>VAT</u> (Value Added Tax) is levied on most goods bought in the UK.

- Taxation can be used for <u>social</u> purposes by the government, e.g. raised on products such as alcohol and tobacco, partly to discourage people from using these products.

> **EXAMINER'S TOP TIP**
> When referring to the UK economy, you may have to distinguish between monetary policy and fiscal policy.

Exchange rates

- The exchange rate shows the value of one currency against another.
- Although exchange rates will vary over time, it is normally policy to try and keep a broadly <u>stable</u> exchange rate.
- Rising exchange rates mean lower costs for importers, but exporters suffer from higher prices.
- Under a <u>floating</u> exchange rate system, the price of the currency is set by market forces of supply and demand. Floating exchange rates should solve any balance of payments problems, for example:

Balance of payments deficit = increased imports and lower exports

↓

Demand for, and thus the price of, sterling falls

↓

Import prices are therefore raised, and export prices fall

> **EXAMINER'S TOP TIP**
> Remember that government policies affect different firms in different ways.

- Floating exchange rates may encourage <u>speculation</u> where capital speculators buy currencies, gambling on future changes in their exchange rates.
- Fluctuations in exchange rates can cause problems for businesses. A rising exchange rate causes a loss of competitiveness for exporters, and affects profit margins; a falling exchange rate hits importers. Either way, <u>uncertainty</u> is created.
- A fixed exchange rate, where rates are 'pegged' against each other, helps overcome these uncertainties: an example is the creation of a <u>single currency</u> (the euro) when <u>European Monetary Union</u> was established in most EU countries.

Quick test

1. **State three ways in which inflation and excess demand can be controlled.**
2. a **What is the 'MPC'?**
   b **What is the role of the MPC?**
3. **Distinguish between:**
   a **monetary and fiscal policy**
   b **direct and indirect taxes.**
4. **How does the act of raising taxes reduce spending power?**
5. **What is the difference between a fixed and a floating exchange rate?**

1. Increasing interest rates, increasing taxes, cutting government spending. 2. a) This is the Monetary Policy Committee. b) Its role is to determine, independently of the government, interest rates in order to control inflation. 3. a) Monetary policy is based on interest rates, and fiscal policy on taxes. b) Direct taxes are based on income, and indirect taxes on spending. 4. Raising taxes (whether direct or indirect) effectively takes money from people and businesses. 5. A fixed rate occurs when governments agree to 'peg' their exchange rates against each other; a floating rate is set by the movements of supply and demand.

Inflation and unemployment

- **Inflation is caused by a combination of too much demand for goods and services in the economy, and scarce resources.**
- **'Too much demand' creates <u>demand–pull inflation</u>, because this excess demand cannot be matched by enough supply.**
- **<u>Cost–push</u> inflation is created when costs of production (e.g. wages not supported by productivity) increase.**
- **<u>Rising import costs</u> resulting from a falling pound can also cause inflation to rise.**

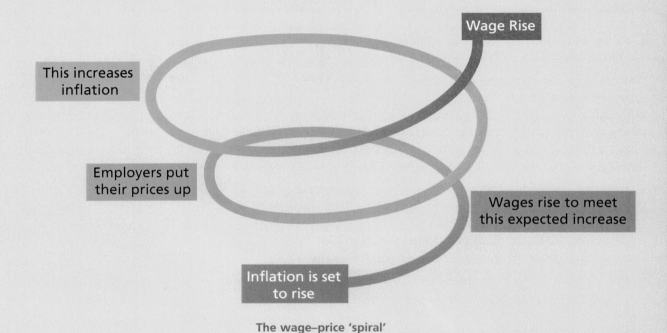

Wage Rise

This increases inflation

Employers put their prices up

Wages rise to meet this expected increase

Inflation is set to rise

The wage–price 'spiral'

- **Inflation therefore affects the <u>behaviour</u> and the <u>survival</u> chances of firms.**
- **Expectations of inflation may lead to firms buying goods now to save costs, increasing their stock levels but also increasing demand and therefore adding to inflationary pressures.**
- **Employees may also seek pay rises as a result of expected inflation.**

The Retail Price Index (RPI)

- The RPI is often used to measure inflation.
- It is based on data collected about buying habits.
- The **prices** of typical goods and services bought are **weighted** according to their relative importance in this typical 'basket' of purchases.
- An **index** is prepared, showing how the total price of the items in the basket is changing.
- As a result, prices can be compared over time.
- However, since the RPI is based on the 'typical' shopping basket of goods, it does not represent inflation for those consumers who have different spending patterns.

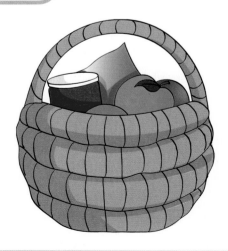

Unemployment

- Governments have <u>full employment</u> as one of their key economic objectives, because unemployment means that scarce economic resources are not being fully used. Rates of unemployment vary tremendously across the UK

Types of unemployment

Structural:	Frictional:
the structural decline of industries, e.g. the shift from manufacturing to tertiary employment, and the effect of substituting capital (machines) for labour	due to the movement between jobs; linked to the **geographical** and **occupational** immobility of labour
Seasonal:	**Cyclical:**
found in heavily seasonal industries such as tourism, where staff are employed for 'the season' only	unemployment arising from the effects of the trade cycle, e.g. when firms reduce labour in a recession

- <u>Geographical</u> immobility of labour occurs when unemployed people are unwilling or unable to move areas to take up work. Social ties, and high living costs in parts of the UK, are common causes.
- <u>Occupational</u> immobility of labour arises from the unwillingness of people to retrain for other work, or the inability to learn new skills. There are certain 'skills shortage' areas in the UK, and a surplus of unskilled or semi-skilled labour.

EXAMINER'S TOP TIP
Inflation is best defined as a fall in the buying power of money, and not as a rise in prices.

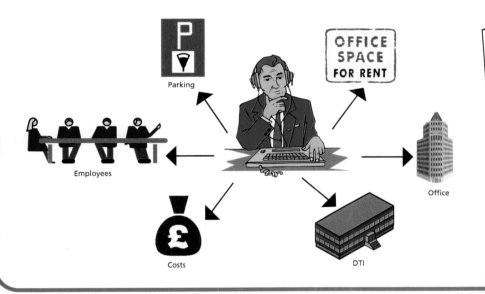

FOR SALE
Detached House
£500 000

EXAMINER'S TOP TIP
In questions about economic policy, remember that any policy changes by the government take time to affect the economy.

Quick test

1 *Distinguish between 'demand–pull inflation' and 'cost–push' inflation.*

2 *Suggest one way that rising inflation can affect the behaviour of a firm.*

3 *What does the RPI show?*

4 *Give one economic reason why the UK government should be concerned about unemployment.*

5 *State how the following arise:*

   a *frictional unemployment*

   b *structural unemployment.*

1. demand–pull: more demand than supply, causing prices to rise; cost–push: increasing costs push up prices
2. e.g. firms may buy now to save costs, if they expect prices to rise in the future
3. how the prices in the 'basket' change over time   4. e.g. because unemployment means scarce economic resources are not being fully used
5. a) as a result of changing jobs   b) due to the decline of some industries

UK and EU law

Sources of law

- In recent years, the UK has established most of its law relating to business by passing 'statute law' through Acts of Parliament.
- The Common Law, interpreted by judges, is another important source.
- Since joining the European Union, EU Regulations and Directives have become an increasing influence on UK businesses.

- A Regulation applies directly in all member states, and if there is a conflict between it and national law, the Regulation prevails.
- A Directive also binds a member state, but how to implement the Directive is left up to the member state.

The Office of Fair Trading (OFT)

The OFT:
- protects consumers from trade practices that are against their interests

- investigates anti-competitive trade practices and any abuse of market power
- encourages competitive behaviour in markets.

Health and safety

- EU member states have harmonised health and safety provisions, to ensure employers adopt safe practices. In the UK, the Health and Safety at Work Act (HASAWA) 1974 sets obligations for employers and employees.
- Employers must provide:
  - safe working environments, processes, plant and systems of work, entry and exit arrangements
  - training and instruction on health and safety.

- Employees must:
  - co-operate on health and safety matters
  - take reasonable care of themselves and others at work
  - not interfere with anything provided for their safety
  - report defects in workplace equipment and processes.

Employee protection

- In addition to health and safety legislation, employees are protected in a number of other ways. One important area is equality of opportunity.
- The Race Relations Acts make it unlawful for an employer to discriminate on grounds of race, colour, nationality and ethnic origin.
- The Sex Discrimination Acts make it unlawful for employers to discriminate on grounds of sex when advertising for and recruiting staff, when promoting them and when setting retirement dates.
- The Disability Discrimination Act 1995 makes it unlawful for disabled persons to be treated less favourably than others.
- The Equal Pay Act 1970 requires employers to pay the same rate to men and women doing the same work.

- Other examples of employee protection include:
  - The EU's Working Time Regulations 1998 establishes, with some exceptions, a maximum average weekly working time of 48 hours, and sets minimum rest and annual leave periods.
  - The Part-time Work Directive ensures part-time staff receive equal treatment with full-time staff.
  - Staff employed under a contract of service are protected against unfair dismissal. They must also be provided with written particulars of their contract of employment within three months of starting work.

Consumer protection

- The <u>Sale and Supply of Goods Act</u> 1994 consolidated previous Acts related to selling goods, which must be:
  - fit for their intended purpose
  - of satisfactory quality
  - as described (if sold by description).
- The <u>Trade Descriptions Acts</u> 1968 and 1972 make it a criminal offence to make a false description of a good or service.

- Other Acts protect consumers in the areas of <u>food safety</u> and <u>weights and measures</u>.
- EU Directives have the purpose of setting common levels of consumer protection throughout the EU. Examples include protection in the areas of product packaging, safety and labelling, price indication, advertising, consumer health, and electronic commerce.

Protection against unfair practices

- EU and UK policy is to get rid of monopolies and unfair trading practices, which are regarded as being against the public interest. Trade between member states should be based on <u>free and fair competition</u>. Examples include the following.
  - The EU controls the use of <u>subsidies</u> by member states, to prevent free trade being distorted.
  - The UK's <u>Competition Act</u> 1998 prohibits cartels and restrictive practices.

- The <u>Enterprise Act</u> 2002 gives new powers to the OFT, and contains provisions dealing with mergers and investigations into markets.

The influence of law on business

- Meeting the demands of consumer and other laws will cost firms money. Firms also benefit from these laws. These benefits include:
  - <u>protection</u>, e.g. against unfair advertising by competitors
  - making <u>competitors meet similar costs</u>, e.g. all firms competing in the food industry cannot avoid hygiene-related costs
  - helping to guarantee the firm's <u>product is saleable</u> (e.g. ensuring it is safe)
  - <u>organising</u> activities efficiently, e.g. to avoid accidents and incidents, which will reduce the need to go to court or attend tribunals.

> **EXAMINER'S TOP TIP**
> You may be asked to explain either how firms **benefit** from existing laws, or how these laws **influence** their actions.

Quick test

1 *Identify three ways in which legal protection influences the environment within which a firm operates.*

2 *State two ways in which HASAWA affects the employer.*

3 *Outline one way in which each of the following Acts encourages equality of opportunity in the workplace:*

 a *Sex Discrimination Act*

 b *Disability Discrimination Act*

 c *Equal Pay Act.*

1. Protects their employees; ensures customers benefit from health and safety protection; protects the firm against unfair competition.
2. Needs to provide safety training; needs to provide safe work practices. 3. a) Employers can't discriminate between men and women when recruiting staff. b) Employers must give disabled people equality of opportunity, such as promotion. c) Employers must pay men and women the same rate of pay for doing the same job.

Issues affecting industry

Stakeholder groups

- A stakeholder group has some link with a firm – the stakeholder group either influences the firm, or is influenced by it. Stakeholders can be either internal, external or both (such as some shareholders).
- Nowadays, many firms recognise the importance of the stakeholder concept, and try to meet the needs and wishes of the various stakeholder groups. Examples include:
  - working with suppliers, e.g. to improve communication and delivery times
  - helping individual and groups of employees by improving working conditions and the quality of working life
  - recognising the value of developing links and improving relationships with the local community.

Internal and external stakeholders

> 'We've always known that as well as providing the right products, a sustainable retail business needs the support of healthy communities and a high quality environment ... We aim to be the most trusted retailer wherever we trade by demonstrating a clear sense of social responsibility and consistency in our decision making and behaviour.'
>
> **Extract from Marks & Spencer plc's Corporate Social Responsibility Statements**

- Benefits to a firm from adopting the stakeholder concept include a motivated workforce, and positive publicity and media coverage.
- One problem of adopting this concept is in reconciling the different objectives that the different stakeholder groups may have: e.g. profitability (investors) with higher pay (employees); lower pollution levels (local community) with quick or inexpensive working methods (managers).

Environmental issues

- Firms are affected by many environmental issues, including global warming, pollution and recycling. As a result, most large firms have their own environmental policies that will influence the work of their various business functions, as shown in the table opposite.

> 'Traffic congestion and the resultant pollution is a major environmental issue ... We are committed to trying to limit the amount of traffic on our roads.'
>
> **Marks & Spencer plc's Corporate Social Responsibility Statements**

Environmental issues continued

Function	Example of influence of environmental policy
Finance	may cause an increase in costs, which must be financed; may obtain investment from environmentally conscious sources
Marketing	helps to define the nature of advertising and promotion used; creates a positive 'consumer-friendly' image for the products
Production	raw materials are chosen with the environment in mind; production processes are less harmful to the environment
HR	staff become prouder and more satisfied working for the firm; may encourage more (qualified/able) people to apply for jobs.

- Although many firms recognise the value of having environmental policies, EU and UK legislation and organisations also exist to protect the environment.
- An example is the **Environment Agency** for England and Wales. This body helps firms comply with Regulations, and to avoid pollution. This could be by advising firms on the EU's Solvents Directive 1999 (which seeks to reduce air pollution), or by ensuring the Control of Pollution (Oil Storage) Regulations 2001 are implemented.

Technological issues

- The work of some industries has been heavily influenced by technological change. Examples include:
  - **Internet-based selling** (e.g. books, insurance, holidays)
  - **computer-aided design** of products.
- Although improved technology comes at the cost of increased investment, the benefits from these technological developments include:
  - **reduced running costs** as a result of more efficient processes and/or fewer staff; and
  - **improved customer satisfaction** through higher quality and reliability.

EXAMINER'S TOP TIP
Remember that all shareholders are stakeholders, but not all stakeholders are shareholders.

EXAMINER'S TOP TIP
Use the major companies' websites to get up-to-date statements on environmental and other issues.

Quick test

1 *Explain the term 'stakeholder group'.*

2 *List two internal and two external stakeholders for a large supermarket.*

3 *Identify, for a large supermarket, one objective that the store's staff may have, and one that the local community may have, that may prove difficult for the store to reconcile.*

4 *Outline how a policy of 'buying cheap' at the expense of protecting the environment may disadvantage a firm having this policy.*

1. a group that has some link with a business   2. internal: e.g. management, staff; external: e.g. competitors, customers, suppliers, government   3. Staff request more parking/better access; The local community does not want the roads to be altered/congestion while alterations are taking place   4. Although costs may be lower, poor publicity may discourage consumers from buying the products even if they appear to be value for money, thereby affecting the firm's sales and therefore its profits.

Social and ethical issues

- Nowadays, businesses are aware of the influence of a positive image on their success in the market-place. These businesses also realise the responsibilities they have to key stakeholder groups. These responsibilities include:
  - following appropriate health and safety policies
  - acknowledging the importance of equality of opportunity
  - having an ethical trading policy; and
  - being environmentally conscious.

'We believe that a business has the responsibility to protect the environment in which it operates, locally and globally... We consider testing products or ingredients on animals to be morally and scientifically indefensible... To meaningfully contribute to local, national and international communities in which we trade, by adopting a code of conduct which ensures care, honesty, fairness and respect.'

Extract from The Body Shop's website

Business ethics

- 'Ethics' refers to the behaviour adopted by a firm. A firm's ethical behaviour is influenced by its corporate (or business) culture.
- It is often set out in the form of an ethical code of practice, a document outlining how the firm and its employees will act:

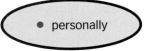 personally
 socially
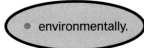 environmentally.

'Marks & Spencer does not manufacture or sell armaments, pornographic material, tobacco products or nuclear power. Neither are we involved in any aspect of animal testing or the provision of gambling facilities ... In the last three years we have not made any political donations or been subject to legal actions on the grounds of health & safety or environmental compliance ...'

Extract from Marks & Spencer plc's Ethical Investment Statement

EXAMINER'S TOP TIP
Check company websites to obtain details of their ethical codes of conduct.

Having an ethical code of practice

Advantages	Disadvantages
More motivated staff	Higher costs (wages, training, etc.)
+ satisfied consumers	+ difficulty in implementing the policy
+ positive media coverage	= reduced profits/profitability
= improved trading prospects	

Pressure groups

EXAMINER'S TOP TIP
When answering questions about pressure groups, concentrate on business issues, i.e. how a group influences the strategy and policies of business.

- These are organised groups of people who share a similar interest, and who wish to influence how others (e.g. government) view this area of interest.
- Pressure groups range in size from local groups interested in local issues to international organisations. Examples include:
  - **ASH** – Action on Smoking and Health
  - **RAC** – the Royal Automobile Club
  - **NCDL** – the National Canine Defence League
  - **TUC** – the Trades Union Congress.
- Pressure groups often campaign in the areas of the <u>environment</u>, <u>employee rights</u>, <u>consumer protection</u>, <u>animal protection</u> and <u>global issues</u> such as debt reduction in developing countries.
- A pressure group can influence the behaviour of firms in several ways. A firm may:
  - take legal or other action to protect its reputation against criticism by a pressure group
  - face increased costs by agreeing to adopt policies requested by the pressure group
  - change its products or sources of supply as a result of the pressure group's campaign
  - change its methods if pressure group policies result in a change in regulations or other laws.
- The level of <u>public</u>, <u>political and financial support</u> for the pressure group's aims affects how successful it will be in achieving these aims.

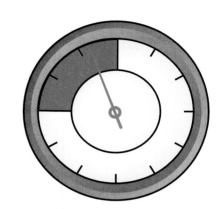

ASH is a campaigning public health charity ... aimed at achieving a sharp reduction and eventual elimination of the health problems caused by tobacco.

Communicating the scale and diversity of the problem to decision makers, the public and the media to create proper understanding of the damaging role of tobacco in society.

Advocacy and lobbying of all relevant stakeholders for practical public policy measures to control tobacco based on evidence and best practice, as well as new ideas.

Networking and alliance-building with a wide variety of organisations interested in health and welfare – especially using the Internet and e-mail communication.

Challenging the tobacco industry's misleading or dishonest information and bogus arguments, and taking action to restrain tobacco companies' damaging conduct.

How we work

Operating at different levels within the UK, through the European Union and internationally to secure our aims in Britain and beyond.

Innovating to ensure our work is as imaginative and fresh as possible.

Extract from ASH Mission Statement (www.ash.co.uk)

Quick test

1. Identify two advantages for a firm that can result from introducing an ethical code of practice.

2. State what a company's ethical code of practice will outline.

3. Name and state the main purpose of one pressure group in each of the following areas:

   a. protection of workers' rights
   b. consumer protection
   c. environmental protection
   d. animal protection.

1. e.g. improved staff motivation, more positive publicity/media coverage, satisfied customers, improved trading prospects 2. How it and its staff will act, e.g. personally, socially and environmentally. 3. a) The NUT (National Union of Teachers) seeks to improve teachers' pay and conditions b) e.g. the Consumers' Association campaigns on consumer issues to do with areas such as food, health and personal finance c) e.g. Greenpeace uses non-violent confrontation to expose global environmental problems d) The Cats' Protection League shelters and seeks to re-home cats and kittens in the UK.

External influences

1 Explain how the study of demand and supply might help a builder of new homes make appropriate business decisions. [6]

....

....

....

....

....

....

2 a Describe the difference between monetary policy and fiscal policy. [2]

....

....

b Explain why both of these measures may be used to control inflation in the UK economy. [4]

....

....

....

....

3 Is increasing demand a good thing or a bad thing for the UK economy? [4]

....

....

....

....

4 Outline the effect on UK exporters to the USA of a fall in the value of sterling against the dollar. [2]

....

....

....

5 Is rising inflation good or bad for UK business? [4]

....

....

....

....

6 a Describe the difference between occupational and geographical immobility of labour. [2]

....

....

....

b Give **one** likely example of each in the UK economy. [2]

....

....

7 Explain why some UK firms may find it difficult to recruit staff even when unemployment
levels in the UK are high. [4]

....

....

....

....

8 Outline, using examples, the general effects that UK and EU law have on business in
this country. [4]

....

....

....

....

9 What forms of discrimination are still found in the workplace, and how does the UK seek to
overcome them? [6]

....

....

....

....

....

10 Illustrate **three** ways in which major retailers such as Sainsbury's and ASDA might be
influenced by the actions of their consumers. [6]

....

....

....

....

....

Total: /46

Starting a business

Entrepreneurs

- An entrepreneur is a risk-taker who takes risks in order to gain the reward of <u>profits</u>. Entrepreneurs are therefore <u>business decision-makers</u>, one of the four <u>factors of production</u>. The others are:
  - <u>land</u>, for which the reward is <u>rent</u>
  - <u>labour</u>, for which the reward is <u>wages</u>; and
  - <u>capital</u>, for which the reward is <u>interest</u>.

- The entrepreneur will need to obtain <u>finance</u>: for sole traders and partners, this often takes the form of personal savings, or cash generated from the sale of personal assets such as a house. Limited companies can sell shares, either direct to the public (PLCs) or to nominated individuals (private limited companies).

Acts as a reward to the entrepreneur ← **PROFIT** → Allows the entrepreneur to expand the firm

Encourages other entrepreneurs to enter the market

Increases competition and keeps prices down

Provides greater consumer choice

Profit

- Three other important factors when starting a business are:

| identifying <u>suitable goods or services</u> for which there is a gap in the market | deciding <u>where to locate</u> | choosing the <u>form of the business</u> |

EXAMINER'S TOP TIP
Remember that more than one person can actually work in a sole-trader business.

Sole traders and partnerships

- A <u>sole trader business</u> consists of a single owner. As with a partnership, a sole-trader business is <u>unincorporated</u>: it does not have a legal identity different to the owner, and it suffers from <u>unlimited liability</u> whereby the owner may have to use personal wealth to meet business debts.

- The traditional <u>partnership</u> business is also unincorporated and unlimited. Like a sole trader, a partnership:
  - is easy and inexpensive to establish
  - can keep its financial affairs relatively private.

- Partnerships, when compared with sole traders, normally find it easier to obtain additional capital, and can share the burden of work; however, decisions must be agreed, and profits must be shared.

−		+
are often small, and any losses are borne by the sole trader	**PROFITS**	do not have to be shared with others
capital is not easy to obtain and cannot be obtained from a share issue	**SETTING UP**	little capital is needed, and there are few formalities
the burden is not shared with others; typically long hours and little chance of holidays	**CONTROL**	easy to keep overall control, and be 'your own boss'
might have to be made without assistance	**DECISIONS**	can be made quickly

Features of the sole trader

Limited companies

- The <u>private limited</u> company, being incorporated, is a <u>separate legal entity</u> from its owners (shareholders) who gain from <u>limited liability</u>.
- Unlike a <u>public limited</u> company (PLC), a private company cannot sell its shares directly to the public, so it is usually smaller with less capital, although its affairs are more private since it does not have to publish its accounts.
- In the UK, many <u>multinationals</u> are in the form of PLCs.

> **EXAMINER'S TOP TIP**
> Be careful to distinguish between public and private sectors, and public and private companies.

Other forms of ownership

- <u>Franchises</u> use the name and logo of an existing company. Well-known examples include many 'fast food' outlets.
  The <u>franchisee</u> buys and runs the franchise, paying the franchisor company for this right.

The franchisee	The franchisor
receives a nationally recognised product, together with marketing and other specialist support.	can expand without major investment, and has a highly motivated business selling the product.

- Consumer and worker <u>co-operatives</u> are found in the UK economy. Capital and profit are not normally so important, with control often being shared democratically.
- The public sector contains <u>public corporations</u>, subject to state control (e.g. financial targets are often set). Many of the former state corporations have been <u>privatised</u> (taken into private ownership) and <u>deregulation</u> has been used by UK governments to stimulate competition.

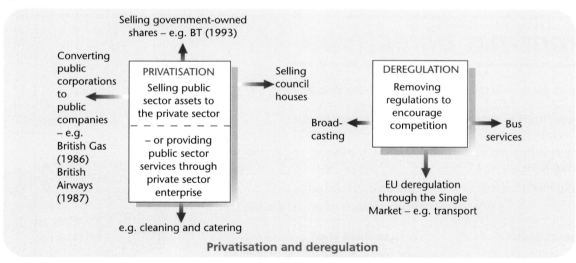

Privatisation and deregulation

Quick test

1 *Give examples of each factor of production for:*

a Vauxhall

b a local dentist's private practice.

2 *State two differences between a sole trader and a partnership.*

3 *State two differences between a private and a public limited company.*

1. a) entrepreneurs – owners; land – factories; labour – workforce; capital – shares   b) entrepreneur – owner of the practice; land – where the surgery is located; labour – hygienists, receptionists; capital – the owner's investment   2. e.g. number of owners; need to have some form of agreement (partnership)   3. e.g. private company cannot ask the public to subscribe for shares, and it does not have to publish its financial statements

Business objectives

Mission statements

- The overall <u>aim</u> and purpose of a business is given in its mission statement. The mission statement is then turned into a series of corporate <u>goals</u> or <u>objectives</u>.

> *'Our mission is to be the consumer's first choice for food, delivering products of outstanding quality and great service at a competitive cost through working "faster, simpler and together".'*
>
> **Mission Statement for Sainsbury's supermarkets**

- **Mission statements often identify a <u>stakeholder</u> – for example, Sainsbury's names its key stakeholder as the consumer.**
- **This allows the business to plan its <u>objectives</u>, and make sure they are focused on meeting the needs of the named stakeholder.**
- **As a result, the business is in a position to create a <u>strategy</u> to achieve its objectives.**

Our mission for Sainsbury's supermarkets

Out-standing quality / Great service / Faster Simpler Together / Competitive cost

→ increasing shareholders returns

Corporate objectives

- Businesses set a wide range of objectives. These include:

(increasing market share)   (profit maximisation)   (growth)   (diversification)

Corporate objective	Value to the firm adopting it
Increasing market share	– more control over price – helps establish future new products
Profit maximisation	– increase share price – meet many shareholders' objectives
Growth	– remain price-competitive – help control the degree of competition
Diversification	– enter new markets to increase profits – spread the risk

EXAMINER'S TOP TIP
Be careful to distinguish between aims, objectives and strategy.

- Corporate objectives should be **measurable** so the business can assess its performance.
- To make them measurable, these corporate objectives are turned into **departmental** or **functional** objectives, which in turn can be developed in detail to become objectives for **individuals** to achieve. **Management by objectives** (MBO) is an approach where managers and staff agree objectives, with the targets set acting as a control mechanism.
- As a result, **appraisal** of individual staff includes assessing whether these personal objectives have been achieved, and what new personal objectives need setting.

The business plan

- Business objectives form the overall business plan, which states what the business seeks to achieve.
- The plan, and its objectives, may be structured into:

short-term objectives:	typically, objectives up to a calendar or financial year ahead	– e.g. to train all office staff to follow the new fire procedure
medium-term objectives:	normally, objectives achievable in between one and five years	– e.g. to ensure all office staff possess the European Computer 'Driving Licence'
long-term objectives:	usually objectives that take longer than five years to achieve	– e.g. to become the market leader in the manufacture and sale of 'home office' furniture

- As with objectives, the business plan can be structured on a departmental or functional basis. The business may therefore have a:
  - **Marketing plan:** e.g. for its products and their 'unique selling point' (USP), promotion policy, pricing structure, distribution, market research
  - **Production plan:** materials to be used, sources of supply, production methods
  - **Human resource plan:** staff recruitment, retention, welfare and training
  - **Financial plan:** sources and amounts required to finance everyday running costs as well as major investment.

Types of business

- Entrepreneurs set up and control **private-sector firms** to make profit from their business activities. These firms may be owned by others: for example, companies being owned by **shareholders**. As a result there can be a '**divorce of ownership and control**':
  - decisions made by the directors (controllers) may clash with the wishes of the shareholders (owners)
  - for example, directors wish to follow a policy of steady growth rather than meet shareholders' wishes for short-term profit maximisation.
- The **public sector** consists of organisations owned and/or financed by central and local government, such as the NHS and the defence agencies. The profit motive, while it may still exist, is far less important, with greater emphasis on providing a **public service**.

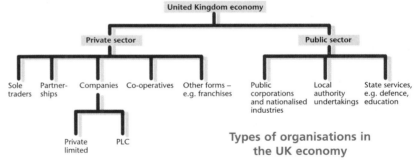

Types of organisations in the UK economy

Quick test

1 Define the term 'mission statement'.

2 Explain the difference between an aim and an objective.

3 Give two likely objectives for a major food retailer.

4 Give one possible example from:

   a the long-term marketing plan of Ford

   b the short-term human resource plan of Asda

   c the medium-term production plan of a local baker.

EXAMINER'S TOP TIP
Use company websites to get more examples of stated aims and plans.

1. A statement of a business's aims, communicated to those inside and outside the business. 2. Aim: an overall, long-term intention of the business in terms of how it will develop; objective: a shorter-term, measurable target the business sets its staff to achieve. 3. To improve staff training so that service to customers is improved; to introduce new equipment to further improve hygiene when cooking and handling food. 4. a) To produce the best-selling large family saloon in the UK. b) To ensure all checkout staff are trained to use new scanning equipment. c) To introduce new baking equipment to gain from power-saving efficiencies.

Business strategy

Strategy and stakeholders

- 'Strategy' refers to a plan of action by which a business tries to achieve its objectives. The plan is based on examining <u>internal</u> and <u>external</u>:

<u>influences</u> on the business | <u>sources of information</u> for the business

- An organisation might find there is conflict in the short term between the objectives of two or more of its stakeholder groups.

- An example would be where shareholders expect short-term, profit-maximising policies to be carried out, whereas employees want improved pay and working conditions – which would increase costs and therefore reduce profits in the short term.

- In the long run, conflicts like this may be resolved if the business strategy results in improved profits, quality, efficiency, and staff welfare: for example, if better working conditions motivate staff to work harder, profits may still increase.

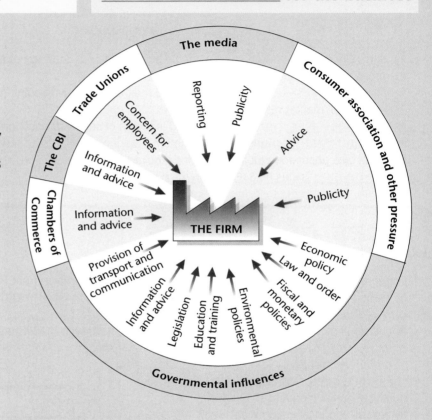

Auditing

- A business may decide to carry out an <u>internal</u> or <u>external</u> audit of its operations.
- Internally, the business will try to identify its own <u>strengths</u> and <u>weaknesses</u>, often using a competitor as a <u>benchmark</u> against which the business can measure itself.
- Externally, the business will assess influences such as the state of the local, national and/or international <u>economy</u>, its position in its <u>market(s)</u>, and the nature and strength of its <u>competition</u>. One way of doing this is to consider undertaking a <u>STEP</u> analysis.
- The information that results from these audits needs organising and analysing under various headings. One popular method of analysis is to carry out a <u>SWOT</u> analysis.

Internal audit	*External audit*
Strengths of the organisation Weaknesses of the organisation	Opportunities in the external environment Threats in the external environment
Internal focus on culture structure leadership styles planning effectiveness	**External focus on** competition and markets social and demographic factors economic and political changes developments in technology

STEP (PEST) analysis

- This analysis helps businesses to assess their markets and influences, and to plan appropriate strategies.

• <u>Social:</u> →	changes in consumer lifestyles, tastes and habits affect demand for products	*– e.g. changing tastes in food such as distrust of GM foodstuffs and increased demand for organically grown food, and more leisure time increasing the demand for holidays*
• <u>Technological:</u> →	improvements in technology affect approaches to production and marketing	*– e.g. more environmentally friendly car engines, faster and more powerful computer 'chips'*
• <u>Economic:</u> →	interest rates and the level of incomes generally will affect the demand for goods and services	*– e.g. a rise in interest rates cuts spending power, so fewer luxury items are likely to be bought*
• <u>Political:</u> →	government taxation and laws influence demand	*– e.g. new consumer protection legislation may affect the way a business markets its products.*

- Other 'letters' are sometimes included to extend the range of 'PEST'. One popular example is to include '<u>E</u>' for <u>environmental</u> issues (PESTE): an example is when new anti-pollution laws affect a firm's production methods.

EXAMINER'S TOP TIP
Distinguish between the use of STEP (external) and SWOT (internal and external) analysis.

SWOT analysis

- This analysis focuses on a firm's <u>Strengths</u> and <u>Weaknesses</u>, which are internal to it, and the <u>Opportunities</u> and <u>Threats</u> that are external.
- For example, a firm that makes and sells double-glazing (doors and windows) might find that carrying out a SWOT analysis identifies the following influences:
  <u>S</u>: good local reputation; well-qualified fitters; windows thought of as good quality
  <u>W</u>: a sales policy that customers regard as rather 'pushy' and too direct; poor-quality door units
  <u>O</u>: possibility of moving to a new factory site that has a more modern layout
  <u>T</u>: local competition from a major national supplier of double-glazing that is marketing heavily in the local area.

EXAMINER'S TOP TIP
Try applying SWOT analysis to a firm that you know.

Quick test

1 *Define the term 'business strategy'.*
2 *Explain the difference between the meaning of the 'S' and 'T' in SWOT and STEP analysis.*
3 *Outline a possible SWOT analysis for:*
  a *a petrol station in a small village*
  b *a kennels and cattery business that looks after pets when their owners go on holiday.*

1. a plan by which a business seeks to achieve its goals   2. S in SWOT is for strengths (internal strengths of the business) and S in STEP is social (changes in society affecting demand for a firm's products). T in SWOT is threats (external threats to the business) and T in STEP is technological (how changes in technology influence the work of a firm).   3. a) e.g. strengths: good service, convenience, many other items sold; weaknesses: employee absenteeism; opportunities: increase the range of items sold; threats: price-cutting major petrol suppliers in a nearby town. b) e.g. strengths: good reputation, open 365 days a year; weaknesses: the site lacks space; opportunities: buy adjoining land to expand; threats: local people objecting to the noise from the dogs

Objectives and strategy

1 In 2001 Natalie Osborne was made redundant from her job. Natalie decided to enter into a franchise agreement with Surprise Fries, a national fast-food chain. The agreement Natalie entered contained a clause that she would only sell food and other products sold to her by Surprise Fries.

   a Suggest **two** other likely clauses that would be in the agreement between Natalie and Surprise Fries. [4]

   ....

   ....

   ....

   ....

   ....

   b Outline the advantages and disadvantages to Natalie of entering into a franchise agreement, rather than setting up her own business to sell fast food. [6]

   ....

   ....

   ....

   ....

   ....

   ....

   ....

   c Suggest **two** reasons why Surprise Fries might find it beneficial to offer franchise outlets rather than set up its own outlets. [4]

   ....

   ....

   ....

   ....

   ....

2 In 2001 Arthur Jefferson was also made redundant from his job as a carpenter. Arthur had always made wooden garden furniture and other items for his friends and family, and so he decided to invest his redundancy savings into setting up his own business. Arthur planned to make wooden benches and chairs for gardens, as well as bird boxes and wooden ornaments. Arthur rented an outlet in a small craft centre where he could make and sell his products, and he advertised his new venture in the local newspaper.

a Suggest **two** likely short-term, and **one** likely long-term, business objectives that Arthur might have set when he started in business. [6]

....

....

....

....

....

....

b Write a simple mission statement for Arthur's business. [4]

....

....

....

3 Give examples of how a national retailer of clothes, such as BHS or Marks & Spencer, could apply STEP analysis to its own situation. [8]

....

....

....

....

....

....

....

4 Mercante Ltd is a private limited company selling plastic casings for warm air heaters and other products. The directors of Mercante Ltd are changing the status of the business to a public limited company. Outline the likely changes in the company's situation, now that it is becoming a PLC. [6]

....

....

....

....

....

....

Total: /38

Marketing strategy

The marketing function

- The purpose of marketing has been defined as getting the <u>right products</u> to the <u>right customers</u> at the <u>right price</u> at the <u>right time</u>. In order to do this, the marketing function of an organisation collects and analyses information about its customers and on its market.

- The traditional production-led business approach – an <u>production-led strategy</u> – concentrated on the product (how easily and efficiently it could be made) rather than what it was about the product that appealed to the customer. A business having a <u>market-led strategy</u>, on the other hand, examines the business's activities through the eyes of its consumers.

- The marketing function in a market-led organisation has three main roles. It:
  - <u>collects and analyses data</u> about the firm's markets and consumers
  - <u>establishes how to market</u> the firm's products
  - <u>co-ordinates the other functions</u> in order that marketing will be successful.

- Most businesses now adopt this 'marketing concept', which puts the customer at the start of the business cycle rather than at its end.

Marketing influence on the business cycle

Influences on the strategy

- A firm's marketing strategy is a long-term plan designed to meet its marketing objectives. The strategy is put into practice through the <u>four Ps</u> of the marketing mix, and is influenced by the firm's:
  - customers – e.g. number, age profile, socio-economic status
  - market locations – e.g. if abroad, language and other cultural influences on packaging and advertising
  - competitors – e.g. policies on price, advertising and promotion, product portfolio ranges
  - products – e.g. whether sold in a <u>niche</u>, or <u>mass</u>, <u>market</u>
  - marketing budget – its size, whether it is increasing or being cut
  - social and environmental policies.

- The following is an example of how marketing strategy can be influenced by environmental concerns:

> **ASDA's Environment Policy**
> 'We recognise that the activities and services we operate can potentially have a negative effect on our natural environment ...
> ASDA is committed to:
> – Minimising packaging on own brand product;
> – Ensuring that packaging volume and weight are limited to the minimum adequate to maintain the necessary level of safety, hygiene and quality for the packed product as well as the aesthetic acceptance of the customer;
> – A key consideration during the packaging design process is to minimise its impact on the environment when packaging is disposed of as waste.'
>
> **Extract from ASDA website**

Marketing objectives

How a product is marketed will be influenced by the marketing objectives of the business. Examples of typical marketing objectives are to:

increase market share to 15% by the end of the financial year

establish the product as the market leader within five years

enter a new market and obtain 5% market share within two years

sell 2 000 products a month through direct selling

develop 35% customer recognition of the new product as a result of the TV advertising campaign

establish 80% brand loyalty for the product through repeat purchases.

The business will need to review how its marketing objectives influence the other functional objectives.

- Influence on **finance**: objectives to increase market share or introduce a new product will have important financial implications, such as the cost of a new advertising campaign.
- Influence on **production**: marketing's objectives for its products – plans about their design, number and availability – will influence how and when production supplies them.
- Influence on **HRM**: an objective to increase market share, or to re-brand a product, will lead to additional staff being needed or existing staff being retrained.

Mass and niche marketing strategies

- **Mass marketing** developed in the early twentieth century: Henry Ford's 'Model T' car is the best-known example. The aim of mass marketing is to achieve market domination through targeting the product at the whole market, rather than at particular consumers.
- Ford's approach to making the Model T illustrates the situation when mass marketing is based on asset-led mass production. Through using economies of scale, he provided a product that many more people could afford than previously, but the product lacked individuality: Ford's best-known quote is that the Model T was available in any colour, 'so long as it's black'.
- **Global marketing** is an extension of mass marketing. Well-known global marketers and brands include Levis, Chanel, Sony, Ford, Coca-Cola, and McDonalds. Although the products are essentially the same in each country, these companies change their pricing and promotional policies from country to country to reflect the local situations:
  - prices tend to be lower in less wealthy countries – e.g. global food and drink brands
  - the product may be modified to cater for cultural, religious, social, legal and other differences –

e.g. right-hand drive cars in the UK, the content and range of global 'fast food'
  - promotion will vary – e.g. the availability of televisions, use of different language and images.

- Global marketing offers the advantage of **increased market size**, as a result of which further economies of scale may be gained. Costs are controlled through **standardising** the product as far as possible, and the product's life-cycle may be extended through marketing globally.
- A **niche-marketing** strategy is when a business chooses to concentrate on a **particular market segment**, rather than trying to appeal to the mass market.

  - The strategy may be followed not only by a specialist firm that is too small to compete successfully with the market leaders, but also by a large company that markets products specifically for a niche market.

EXAMINER'S TOP TIP
Discover examples of products sold in a niche market.

EXAMINER'S TOP TIP
Find examples on company websites of market-led strategies and marketing objectives.

Quick test

1. **List the three main roles of the marketing function.**
2. **Identify three influences on a firm's marketing strategy.**
3. **What is a niche marketing strategy?**
4. **How will a marketing objective to re-brand an existing product influence the HRM function?**
5. **State one way in which a globally marketed product will vary from country to country.**

1. e.g. to collect and analyse customer data; to make decisions about marketing the products; to co-ordinate the other functions. 2. e.g. its customers, its competitors, the size of its marketing budget, its products, its market location. 3. when a firm concentrates on a particular market segment. 4. Existing staff may need retraining to learn about the re-branding. 5. e.g. its price, its packaging, its design, its promotion

Market segmentation

Segmenting the market

- Market segmentation is part of the overall task of target marketing. The purpose of segmenting a market is to divide it into distinct **subgroups**. The basis of the segmentation is usually by **consumer**.
- There are many different bases used to segment consumer markets.

Demographic segmentation – segmenting using consumer characteristics has a number of categories.

- **Age** – Buying behaviour is closely related to age categories for many products.
- **Sex** – Men and women have differing buying habits and needs.
- **Family life cycle** – Consumers may be divided into four categories:
  (1) single adults,
  (2) married adults without children,
  (3) family (at least one child), and
  (4) adults whose children have left home.
- **Social class and income** – Classifications are based on the head of household's occupation, such as:
  - **A** higher managerial and professional – e.g. senior executives
  - **B** intermediate managerial, administrative and professional – e.g. accountants and other members of the 'professions'
  - **C1** supervisory, clerical, junior administrative or professional – e.g. office staff
  - **C2** skilled manual – e.g. electricians, plumbers
  - **D** semi-skilled and unskilled manual – e.g. refuse collectors
  - **E** state pensioners, lowest grade workers – e.g. casual staff, students.

Behavioural segmentation – analysis of how the product is consumed, for example on the basis of **loyalty**:

- hard-core loyals – consumers with complete loyalty to a brand
- soft-core loyals – consumers with divided loyalties between at least two brands
- shifting loyalties – consumers who regularly switch brands
- switchers – consumers with no brand loyalty.

Segmenting the market

Geodemographic segmentation – analysis of the location and type of neighbourhood in which customers live. This analysis is important to industries such as tourism and leisure, influencing, for example, where a new hotel, leisure centre or restaurant is to be located. The **ACORN** (A Classification Of Residential Neighbourhoods) system may be used: an example of ACORN groupings is group B (modern family housing, high income), which is then analysed further (e.g. B6, new detached houses, young families).

Psychographic segmentation – analysis based on the lifestyles, common interests and attitudes of customers that influence their buying habits. Lifestyle segmentation is used to classify which market segments interest particular groups. These groups are sometimes known by their initials, e.g. YUPPIES ('young and upwardly mobile') and DINKY ('double income no kids yet').

- Industrial markets can be segmented, using bases such as the size or location.

EXAMINER'S TOP TIP
Practise applying methods of market segmentation to a range of well-known products.

Analysing the market

EXAMINER'S TOP TIP
Remember that the nature of the market (e.g. consumer or industrial) is a major influence on the type of segmentation used.

- Markets may be classified according to the type of <u>buyer</u>.
- <u>Consumer markets</u> exist for products bought by people:
  - <u>single-use goods</u> – e.g. sweets, cosmetics, food – that have short lives
  - <u>consumer-durable goods</u> – e.g. televisions, DVD players – that are bought less frequently, and which often have an income-elastic demand
  - <u>services</u>, such as electricians, insurance and transport.
- <u>Industrial markets</u> exist for products bought by firms. These are in the form of:

<u>capital goods</u> **such as machines and equipment**

<u>consumables</u> **– e.g. stationery, lubricants**

<u>services</u> **such as cleaning and insurance.**

Feature	Consumer market	Industrial market
Product is likely to be …	standardised, with an attempt to differentiate it from those of competitors	made to customer requirements
Market tends to have …	many customers who take the price	few customers, and price may be negotiated
The distribution channel …	varies according to market size and type	tends to be direct to the final customer

- Markets can also be analysed according to their <u>size</u>. Market size is calculated by measuring the sales for each firm in the market compared to the total sales in the market. The market will also be subject to <u>growth</u>: it may be expanding (e.g. the UK DVD market) or contracting (e.g. the UK videotape market).
- Measuring market size and the rate of growth is important, because it is used as the basis for calculating <u>market share</u>, the proportion of the total market that each firm has. Many firms regard changes in their market share as being one of the key measures of success because it is an indicator of their <u>competitiveness</u> against their rivals.
- Firms also analyse their <u>target market</u>: the consumers at whom they aim their products. To do so, the firm creates a <u>consumer profile</u> – for example, by age, sex, location and socio-economic status. Consumer profiles are used in market segmentation analysis.

Quick test

1 List the three types of goods found in:

   a consumer markets

   b industrial markets.

2 Explain the difference between market size and market share.

3 State the difference between:

   a demographic and geodemographic segmentation

   b behavioural and psychographic segmentation.

1. a) single-use; consumer-durable; services   b) capital goods; consumables; services   2. Market size is a measure of the total sales in the whole market; market share is a measure of an individual firm's sales in the market.   3. a) demographic is by consumer characteristics and geodemographic by consumer neighbourhoods   b) behavioural is by brand loyalty, and psychographic by lifestyle

Marketing research

- Marketing research seeks to collect information about the buying habits of a firm's <u>consumers</u>. It also includes collecting information about the firm's <u>competitors</u>, and the <u>market</u> in general.

The market:
- What is its size, and is it growing or contracting?
- How is it segregated?
- Is it seasonal?

The competition:
- Who are the competitors?
- How large and powerful are they?
- What marketing mix does each competitor use?

Marketing research concentrates on four aspects:

The consumer:
- Who buys it?
- How often do they buy it?
- Why do they buy it?

The product:
- What stage is it at in its life-cycle?
- Can it be modified to extend its life?
- How competitive is its price and promotion?

EXAMINER'S TOP TIP
Market research is often a continuous process, not simply being carried out when a new product is being considered.

Primary and secondary research

<u>Primary</u> research is also known as <u>field research</u>. Primary research uses a range of methods to collect the original data.
- <u>Questionnaires</u> – Designed for the task, these are completed by face-to-face or telephone interview, or through the post.
- <u>Test marketing</u> – The proposed product is marketed in a limited way (e.g. one area of the country), and consumer views are obtained.
- <u>Consumer panels</u> – Consumers receive the product, and give their views on it.
- <u>Retailer interviews</u> – Opinions of the retailers selling the product are obtained.
- <u>Observation</u> – Trained observers record consumer reaction when buying the product.

<u>Secondary</u> research is also known as <u>desk research</u>. This research involves using statistics and other information that is already in existence. One <u>internal</u> source of information is the firm's own records, e.g. of sales made. <u>External</u> information sources include:
- government statistics published by the Office of National Statistics
- information from specialist agencies – e.g. trade associations and publications
- market intelligence reports from market research agencies such as Mintel
- articles and special reports in newspapers and business magazines
- company annual reports and financial statements.
- 'Primary' and 'secondary' are probably better names to use than 'field' and 'desk', because primary and secondary research can both be carried out from a desk.

Primary research	Secondary research
Focuses mainly on the product	Low cost of collection
Up-to-date data is obtained	Is usually quantitative
Opportunity to collect qualitative data	Obtained quickly
But	**But**
More expensive to obtain	Data may be out-of-date
Possible interviewer bias	Much of the data may not be relevant

Marketing research

Quantitative and qualitative research

- Firms undertaking <u>quantitative</u> research want to discover factual information: for example, number sold, percentage sales of different products in the range, amount of market share.
- Firms undertaking <u>qualitative</u> research try to discover consumer attitudes and opinions, likes and dislikes, about the product.

Quantitative questions	Qualitative questions
How many … do you buy?	Why do you buy … ?
Have you heard of … ?	How do you feel about … ?
Which … do you like?	Why do you like … ?

Sampling and market research

- If market research is to provide accurate information, the researchers must identify and use an appropriate <u>sample</u> of consumers, who must therefore accurately represent the market being researched. The firm will need to consider the number of people – the <u>sample size</u> – and how the 'right' people are identified for the sample (the <u>sampling method</u>).
- There are a number of sampling methods available.

<u>Random sampling</u>: everyone in the population has an equal chance of being selected – for example, every fiftieth person on the electoral register is selected.

<u>Stratified sampling</u>: a subgroup of the population is selected – for example, all car owners, all women over the age of 30.

<u>Quota sampling</u>: a quota is set for each target subgroup in the consumer profile – for example, if the profile is 75% male and 25% female, and one-third of the men are under the age of 20, a quarter of all people sampled would be men under 20 (i.e. one-third of 75%).

- Some firms also use either <u>cluster</u> sampling – a random sample that is limited to an area such as a single town – or <u>convenience</u> sampling, which involves sampling from the most convenient area (simple and inexpensive, but often open to bias).
- The firm must therefore balance the higher cost of collecting data from a large sample against the greater accuracy that a larger sample should bring to the results, and therefore to its decision-making.

EXAMINER'S TOP TIP
Remember that the larger the sample size, the more accurate the results are likely to be but the greater the cost to the firm.

Quick test

1 *Name the four aspects that marketing research concentrates on.*
2 *Give one advantage and one disadvantage of using primary research.*
3 *State the difference between quantitative and qualitative research.*
4 *What is the difference between random and stratified sampling?*

views and opinions.   4.   random: everyone has an equal chance of being selected; stratified: a subgroup of the random sample is identified
e.g. collection can be costly and time-consuming   3.   Quantitative researches factual information; qualitative researches into customer
1.   the product; the competition; the market; the consumer   2.   advantage: e.g. the data relates exclusively to the product; disadvantage:

The product life-cycle

- A firm's **product mix** shows the full range of its products in all markets and segments. The mix width identifies the number of lines, and the number of different products in a single product line gives the mix depth.
- **Mix width** indicates the degree of diversification for the firm: the wider the mix width, the more diversified it is, and the greater chance it has of surviving downturns of demand in individual markets or segments. Mix depth indicates how easily the firm can market its products in different segments: the greater the depth, the more likely the firm is to face competition between its own products in any one segment of the market.

EXAMINER'S TOP TIP
Apply product life-cycle analysis to a range of products you know, such as car models, sweets, and computer games.

The life-cycle

- Any product has a limited life once it enters the market. It therefore becomes important for a firm to have a **balanced product portfolio**: one that contains products at different stages of their life-cycle.
- **Product life-cycle analysis** encourages the firm to review its portfolio. It is also used to determine other aspects of marketing strategy, such as how the product is advertised and priced, and the distribution channels to be used. There are four main stages in a product's life-cycle.

The **introduction** stage: after planning and development, the product is introduced into the marketplace. This stage is associated with:
- low initial sales because brand loyalty has not been established
- high costs due to heavy promotion and initial build-up of stocks
- low (if any) profits as a result.

The **growth** stage: sales increase and the firm starts to make profits, as brand loyalty and consumer confidence grow, and economies of scale become possible. If the product is successful, competitors introduce rival products.

The **maturity** stage: the product reaches saturation point and sales level off with profits at their maximum. The firm promotes heavily again, and may try to differentiate the product more clearly from competitors to keep brand loyalty and repeat purchases.

The **decline** stage: sales start to fall. To counter this, the firm may cut the product's price (and therefore its profit margin).

- There is a link between the life-cycle and cash flow.
  - Initially, in the product **development** stage, cash flow will be negative as a result of the capital and other expenditure incurred when planning and developing products.
  - In the initial introduction stage, although cash will be generated from sales, there are still substantial (promotion) costs to be met, so again cash flow may be negative.
  - It is at the maturity stage where large cash inflows are created.
  - Marketing strategies at the decline stage, such as additional advertising and re-packaging, will lead to an increase in cash outflow at a time when inflows are falling as sales fall.

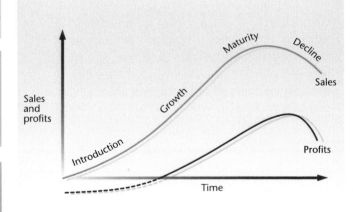

Stages of the product life-cycle

Extending product life

- Product life-cycles are tending to become shorter, as a result of increased competition and developments in technology. As a result, firms may try to extend the life of the product by using **extension strategies**: by doing so, they hope to extend the **maturity** stage of the product, and therefore keep profits at their maximum level.
- The **product** may be altered – new packaging, a new model, a new format (e.g. ice-cream versions of popular chocolate products), finding a new use for the product, cutting its price and changing its name.
- The **marketing strategy** may be altered – e.g. a new image for the product, or a new segment or niche market.

The Boston Matrix

- The Boston Consultancy Group matrix – the 'Boston Box' – analysis is particularly suitable for large companies with a wide product range, and allows the company to analyse its overall **product portfolio**. This product portfolio analysis separates the firm's products into four groups.

- **'Stars'** are those products expected to become highly profitable, so the firm invests heavily in them to turn them into 'cash cows'.

- **'Cash cows'** are those profitable products from which the firm gets the greatest cash flow, so it continues to invest in them.

- **'Problem children'** – also known as **question marks** – are those products marketed in a slow-growth segment, which allow the firm to market a full product range.

- **'Dogs'** are products that use a lot of resources but are still relatively unprofitable, and which will be ended if the firm does not keep making them for strategic or prestige reasons.

Broad links can be established between the stages of the product life-cycle and the Boston Box categories.

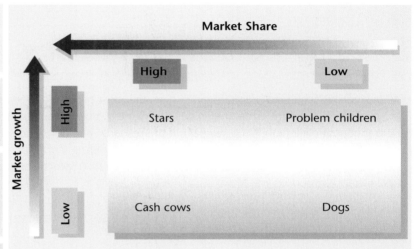

Boston Matrix analysis

Life-cycle stage		Boston Box category
Introduction	⟺	Problem child
Growth	⟺	Star
Maturity	⟺	Cash cow
Decline	⟺	Dog

EXAMINER'S TOP TIP Product life-cycle analysis can be used to analyse individual product brands, and all brands in the same market.

Quick test

1 **Distinguish between a product's mix depth and its mix width.**
2 **What is a 'balanced product portfolio'?**
3 **Identify three popular ways of extending the life of a product.**
4 **Link the stages of the product life-cycle with the Boston Box categories of products.**

1. mix depth: how easily the firm can market its products in different segments; mix width: the number of different products in a single product line 2. one that contains products that are at different stages of the life-cycle 3. a 'new improved' model, a change of name/image, a change of market segment, new packaging, a new format, a new use, a new price 4. introduction = problem child; growth = star; maturity = cash cow; decline = dog

The marketing mix: Product

- Most products are in the form of either goods or services. A person (such as a celebrity) or a place (e.g. a tourist destination) can also be regarded 'a product'.
- A product may be <u>innovative</u>, resulting from a new idea (e.g. the Walkman) or design (e.g. the Dyson cleaner); it may be <u>imitative</u>, copying an existing idea or design; or it may be a <u>replacement</u> product such as the Mini car, taking over from an earlier model.
- The <u>nature</u> of the product influences how it is marketed. A product often serves more than one function for consumers: for example, any car can take a consumer from A to B. However, marketers realised that cars are products that also please consumers in other ways, and they are therefore marketed on the basis of their image, functionality, speed, environmental friendliness, or safety features.

> **EXAMINER'S TOP TIP**
> The 'four Ps' – product, place (distribution), promotion and price – are analysed separately, but they must be combined efficiently if an organisation's marketing strategy is to work.

Developing new products

- All businesses seek new products, since even the most profitable product is likely to move from maturity into decline at some stage. They are interested in developing new products to obtain or keep a <u>competitive advantage</u>.
- New product development is a key part of the research and development (R&D) process. <u>Research</u> explores the possibility of making the product, and <u>development</u> turns this research into the actual product. It is usually only the larger companies that can afford to meet the costs of R&D, which can therefore become an economy of scale if the R&D is successful.

New product development

- <u>Test marketing</u> is an important stage in new product development. Its purpose is to copy as closely as possible real market conditions.
- <u>Screening</u> of products takes place at the test marketing stage. Screening:
  - ensures the product is compatible with the firm's strategy and with other products in the portfolio
  - analyses labour costs, likely competitor reaction, the product's profit potential and its expected length of life-cycle.
- Product development does not only occur at the new product stage. A product may change throughout its life, in an attempt to extend its life, or as a response to the actions of competitors.

Managing existing products

- Most products fail either before or shortly after launch. It is therefore in an organisation's interest to protect its successful products. The organisation can do this by:
  - taking out a patent, which protects the product from being copied by rivals
  - creating a trade mark that distinguishes the product from competing products.
- Certain products have specialist protection available: for example, published works are protected by UK copyright laws from being duplicated without the author's permission.

Product differentiation and branding

- Product differentiation examines <u>how consumers view products</u>. Organisations attempt to <u>differentiate</u> their products as much as possible: a differentiated product is regarded as <u>distinct</u>, and helps the firm make advertising and other marketing strategies more effective. The difference in the product may be real, or it may be perceived as different, e.g. due to effective packaging or advertising.
- Product differentiation is helped if the product has a <u>unique selling point</u> (USP), around which the firm can plan its marketing strategy. The USP may be a real or a perceived difference that makes the product 'unique' from its competitor products.
- <u>Branding</u> guarantees to the customer that the next product bought will be (almost) identical to their last purchase. As a result, <u>brand loyalty</u> can be established and built up.
- Particular brand names have become so well known that they are now used to describe all products of the same type: e.g. Biro (ball-point pen) and Hoover (vacuum cleaner).
- Once a popular brand has been established:
  - the firm can use the resulting goodwill to help market new products
  - repeat purchases are guaranteed
  - retailers are more likely to devote space to promote and sell the brand
  - market segmentation becomes possible.
- <u>Own-label brands</u> are an important feature of modern-day retailing. The retailer buys from a manufacturer, who may also make some of the leading product brands, once quality has been agreed.

'Six own-label brands are offered in ASDA. These have been developed to meet specific customer needs and make up 'ASDA Brand', ASDA's own-label offering. These are:

– *Smartprice: a range of lowest priced food and general merchandise essentials*

– *ASDA brand: a range of 'best in market' everyday food and general merchandise items at ASDA Price, satisfying our customers' shopping needs*

– *Good for you!: a credible range of great tasting foods with lower fat content than standard ASDA Brand alternatives*

– *Organic: a range of best value organic 'everyday' products making organics an acceptable and affordable choice for all the family*

– *Extra Special: ASDA's premium food brand*

– *More For Kids: a range of healthier, fun products for kids across Food, Health & Beauty.'*

Extract about own brands from ASDA website

> **EXAMINER'S TOP TIP**
> Memorise some examples of popular branded products that have been successfully differentiated from their rivals.

Quick test

1 *Give one reason why only large companies tend to undertake major research and development.*

2 *State why test marketing is important to a firm.*

3 *Explain the term 'USP'.*

4 *State one advantage that branding brings to the:*

  a *buyer*

  b *seller.*

1. The process is very costly and may not bring any rewards, so smaller businesses may not be able to afford or risk carrying it out. 2. So that real market conditions can be copied as closely as possible. 3. Unique Selling Point – some feature of a product that differentiates it from its rivals. 4. a) guarantee of the same quality b) repeat purchases through customer loyalty, helps in marketing segmentation

35

The marketing mix: Place

Channels of distribution

- **The channel of distribution refers to the <u>route</u> that is taken by the product, from the producer to the final consumer. In getting the product to the final consumer, a number of distribution costs have to be met. These include:**
  - **transport costs such as petrol, driver's wages, vehicle depreciation**
  - **insurance costs for goods in transit**
  - **warehousing costs, e.g. rent, business rates, staff wages**
  - **costs of protecting the goods in transit, e.g. packaging.**

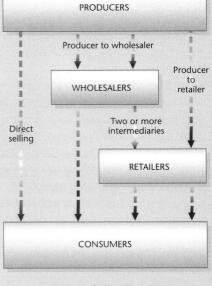

Chain of distribution

The Distribution chain

- The <u>**full distribution chain**</u> of producer–wholesaler–retailer–consumer is still used, often where many small retailers are involved. The wholesaler, whose traditional role is to <u>**break bulk**</u>, acts as a communication link between producer and retailer and provides product information. The use of a wholesaler makes wide product distribution possible without the producer having to meet large transport and other distribution costs.
- The <u>**producer–wholesaler–consumer**</u> channel is widely used by smaller producers who make a limited range of products. By using wholesalers, the producer:
  - has a guaranteed market because the wholesaler bears the risk of the goods not selling to the final consumer
  - reduces stockholding costs, since the wholesaler stores the product
  - receives advice on market performance from the wholesaler.
- The wholesaler is also involved in promoting the product. Compared with direct selling, however, the producer receives lower profit margins, and loses some control over how the product is sold.
- The <u>**producer–retailer–consumer**</u> link is an alternative to the wholesaler channel, and is often used by large-scale retailers such as Tesco and Sainsbury's. The retailer buys the products from its suppliers, and organises its own distribution through its own regional distribution centres. These centres replace the wholesaler, carrying out the key functions of breaking bulk and distributing to the retailer's outlets in the centre's region. Another example is the '<u>**tied outlet**</u>' approach favoured by, for example, petrol companies and breweries.
- Some products are sold <u>**direct from producer to consumer**</u>. Many industrial goods are sold this way, and in the consumer market the 'factory shop outlet' and mail order are popular examples. In using this channel, the seller:
  - reduces costs by avoiding the use of intermediaries such as wholesalers
  - has close contact with the final consumer, and therefore obtains feedback on product performance quickly and easily.
- There can be other organisations employed in the channel:
  - '<u>**Cash & carry**</u>' stores are alternatives to wholesalers, the main difference being that these outlets usually receive payment immediately.
  - <u>**Agents**</u> are found in certain industries – e.g. entertainment ('ticket agents'), cars, travel and house selling – operating for a commission paid by the seller or the buyer.

EXAMINER'S TOP TIP
Questions on 'place' may test your knowledge of the role and value of wholesalers.

Choice of channel

- All channels of distribution offer a level of effectiveness and efficiency, against which the firm must balance the cost of using the channel. The producer must decide the **best outlets** for the product, and the **best method of delivery** to these outlets.
- The **features** of the product are a major influence on the choice of channel. Products vary: they may be fragile, perishable, heavy, expensive, dangerous or bulky. These features will determine the method of transport and distribution channels used. Other major influences include the **frequency** of delivery needed, and the **number** of products involved.
- The firm will assess the degree of **control** it needs over the outlet. Many mass-marketed items are sold through outlets where the marketer is not greatly concerned about the **image** of the outlet. However, with many products that are classified as 'exclusive' or are technologically advanced, the marketer is likely to be more concerned about the outlet's quality and image, and will therefore wish to exert greater control over how the outlet deals with the products.

EXAMINER'S TOP TIP

Study and memorise examples of how companies distribute their products.

Distributing via the Internet

- **E-commerce** is a major growth area. Internet-based distribution can allow a business greater (24-hour) and closer access to, and involvement with, its customers.
- Many products, for example DVDs, CDs and books, are increasingly being distributed from seller direct to buyer as a result of customers using the Internet.

ASDA.com

'Launched in 1998, our home shopping service brings convenience and Always Low Prices to the customer, from the comfort of their own home. Currently operational in 32 stores across the country, with coverage growing constantly, ASDA.com is available to anyone with Internet access.

Registering with ASDA.com is simple and with a range of over 14,000 food and non-food products that is continually being expanded, shopping couldn't be easier.

We recognise that the first online shop can often be the trickiest so our 'Quickstart' system means that all a first-time user has to do is input a few key pieces of information from their last ASDA receipt and the system will download these products as a permanent favourites list.

The customer chooses a time for delivery that is convenient, places their order and pays for their shopping using our 100% secure servers.

Shopping is "picked" by our specially trained colleagues in-store and is delivered by our very own Customer Service Assistants in dedicated temperature-controlled vans between 10am and 10pm.'

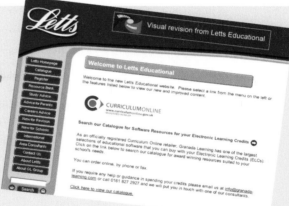

Extract from ASDA website

Quick test

1 **Name three costs associated with distribution.**
2 **State two services that wholesalers provide for:**
   a **retailers**
   b **manufacturers.**
3 **List the four main distribution channels.**
4 **What are the two questions a producer must ask when choosing a distribution channel?**

1. e.g. transport (e.g. petrol), insurance, vehicle depreciation. 2. a) breaking bulk, providing product information b) storage, promoting the product. 3. producer–consumer; producer–wholesaler–consumer; producer–retailer–consumer; producer–wholesaler–retailer–consumer 4. What is the best outlet (channel) for my product? What is the best distribution method to deliver to the relevant outlets?

The marketing mix: Promotion

Promotional strategy

- Firms need to promote their products in order to tell customers about them, and to sell them in a competitive marketplace. This may involve promoting the product in its existing market, or in a new segment or market.

- Firms also promote themselves, in order to improve corporate image in the hope of boosting sales of their products, or to counter any negative publicity received.

- The balance between cost and effectiveness determines the promotional mix that is selected and used by a firm. This mix consists of:
  - 'above the line' promotion – advertising
  - 'below the line' promotion – sales promotion, personal selling.

- The effectiveness of promotion can be analysed using the AIDA technique. The promotional technique must:
  - create an Awareness of the product amongst potential consumers
  - arouse consumer Interest
  - stimulate a Desire to have the product
  - provoke Action by the consumer to purchase it.

- Another way to measure effectiveness is to assess promotional elasticity: the extent to which changes in spending on promotion affect demand for the product. If a small change in (typically) advertising expenditure results in a large increase in products sold, then the product is said to be advertising-elastic.

EXAMINER'S TOP TIP
Remember that much of the advertising we see contains both informative and persuasive elements.

The advertising message

- Advertising is defined as a media-delivered message that is paid for by the sponsor of the message (the advertiser). This differentiates advertising from **publicity**, which is not paid for.
- **Informative advertising** is factually based, the main purpose of the advertising being to provide information about the product.
- The objective of **persuasive advertising** is to tempt consumers into buying the product, persuading them that they 'need' it. This advertising is often based on persuading the consumer to buy the firm's brand, rather than that of a rival. It therefore relies on **branding** and other forms of **product differentiation**, allowing the advertisers to focus on what makes the product being advertised 'different' from the rest.
- Persuasive advertising can therefore create **brand loyalty**, but may be criticised for making outlandish claims and attempting to manipulate consumers by persuading them to buy products they do not need, and may not really want.
- In practice, advertising is **controlled**. This control may be through:
  - legislation such as the EU's Misleading Advertising Directive, and the Trade Descriptions Act
  - the work of bodies such as the Advertising Standards Authority, an independent body for non-broadcast adverts, sales promotions and direct marketing, which administers a code to ensure that adverts are legal, decent, honest and truthful.
- Nowadays, more and more organisations are becoming **ethically aware**, adopting advertising campaigns designed to avoid criticism.

DVD offer

Public relations

- Many large companies have specialist public relations (*PR*) departments, whose role is to ensure that the company's name and products are associated with positive publicity wherever possible.
- The PR department may be involved in designing image-based **corporate advertising** to promote the company's good name.

The advertising medium

- Larger organisations are able to afford the expertise of a <u>specialist advertising agency</u> to create advertising campaigns for them. The organisation or agency has a range of advertising media from which it can choose.
- Commercial national and regional <u>television</u> stations provide <u>mass-market coverage</u> but at a high price (especially peak-time national television), and the advert is not in a permanent form, nor is there any guarantee that potential consumers will not 'channel hop' and miss the adverts completely.
- Commercial national and local <u>radio</u> stations also provide mass coverage, at a lower cost than television though the persuasive impact of moving images is lost, and the advert is still in a temporary form.
- <u>Print-based</u> advertising media allow the advertiser to produce adverts in a permanent and more detailed form – perhaps including a contact address or reply slip with the advert. Advertisers can also target certain groups, by selecting appropriate newspapers or specialist magazines, and the adverts can be inexpensive (in local newspapers). However, the impact of sound and movement is again lost.
- <u>Direct marketing</u> is a popular method of print-based advertising, where leaflets and 'mail shots' are posted through letterboxes. Although relatively inexpensive, there is usually a low response rate to this 'junk mail'.
- Other advertising media include the Internet, cinemas, posters, and carrier bags.

Television company	Advertising spend May 2003 (£m)	Market share (%)
ITV	145.0	51.8
C4	58.0	20.7
GMTV	4.6	1.6
Satellite/cable	50.0	17.9
Five	21.5	7.7
S4C	0.8	0.3
Total	279.9	100.0

Source: *The Guardian*, 7 May 2003

TV advertising spend, May 2003

'Below the line' promotion

EXAMINER'S TOP TIP
When asked to choose an advertising medium, make sure your choice is realistic, in terms of cost, for the given firm and product.

- Firms use <u>sales promotion</u> to encourage new buyers to try their products, and to tempt existing buyers to stay with the brand. The main sales promotion techniques therefore <u>encourage initial and repeat purchases</u>, and are:
  - <u>price reductions</u> and <u>premium offers</u> such as the offer of free gifts, money-off coupons, discounts
  - <u>loyalty cards</u> where points are awarded from spending, the points earning discounts or other incentives
  - <u>free product samples</u> such as sachets of shampoo
  - <u>competitions</u> that encourage people to buy the product
  - <u>after-sales service</u>.
- <u>Point-of sale</u> (POS) promotions include all merchandising that takes place at the till or other point of sale.
- <u>Personal (direct) selling</u> allows the firm to target its buyers, individually tailoring its sales message to them. Highly effective, this approach – often associated with industrial goods – can be expensive due to the need to employ a sales force.

Quick test

1 *Give one reason why an organisation might wish to promote itself.*
2 *Suggest two advantages and two disadvantages to a business from using TV as an advertising medium.*
3 *Identify three methods of 'below the line' promotion.*
4 *Outline the difference between direct selling and direct marketing.*

1. e.g. to improve its corporate image with the public; to counter negative publicity   2. advantages: e.g. sound and image can be persuasive; mass audience can be reached; disadvantages: e.g. high cost; no guarantee that the audience will see the advertisement   3. free offers; point-of-sale display; personal selling   4. direct selling: approaching customers directly; direct marketing: mailshots and other forms of printed material sent to customers without personal contact being made

The marketing mix: Price

'Price' is the amount paid for a product. There are many factors that help determine the price set: <u>internal</u> factors such as the cost of manufacture and the objectives of the firm, <u>external</u> factors such as the nature of the market and competition.

The availability of the product, the degree of customer sensitivity to price changes, the nature of competition and the existence of product substitutes are some influences on how important the product's price is seen to be by the firm's customers.

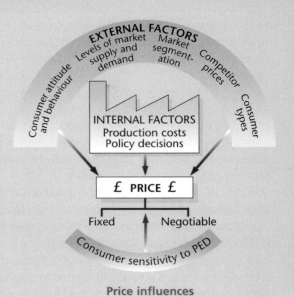

Price influences

Cost-based pricing methods

- The <u>cost-plus</u> method of pricing is based on <u>absorption costing</u>, and takes all the firm's costs into account when setting a price for the product.
  - Direct costs are calculated and allocated to the product.
  - The product's share of the indirect costs (overheads) is calculated, and these are allocated.
  - Total product costs are known, and used to calculate the cost per product.
  - A set margin can then be added to allow for profit and to establish the price.
- One weakness in a pricing policy based on absorption costing is that how the overheads are allocated determines the cost calculations for each product in the product line, and therefore influences its price. Overheads may be apportioned on a very arbitrary basis to a product, which may lead to an inaccurate or unfair price being set.
- In an attempt to overcome the weaknesses of pricing on this cost-plus basis, some firms use <u>contribution</u> pricing. This is based on <u>marginal costing</u> principles, which isolates the firm's fixed costs when setting prices, and calculates the contribution made by each product to the total fixed costs.
- Contribution is calculated as selling price less variable costs.
- The firm can use contribution pricing to set <u>differential</u> prices, for example in the transport industry, where the prices of rail and bus journeys may differ according to the time of day (e.g. 'peak-time' fares), and the age or occupation of the traveller (e.g. student rail pass).
- Cost-based pricing methods ensure the firm's costs are covered and that a profit element is added. However, they may ignore <u>external factors</u> such as the prevailing market price, with which the firm's price needs to be compared.

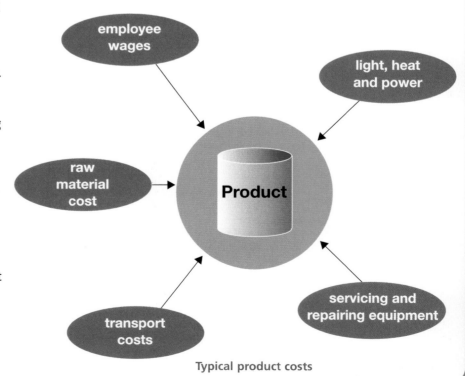

Typical product costs

Market-based pricing

- A firm using market-based pricing takes account of the **market conditions** when setting its prices.
- If the firm is a **price-taker**, it reviews the prevailing market prices and sets its own prices with these in mind. Where there is little product differentiation, and therefore a high price elasticity of demand, the firm must set a price that is competitive.
- The **price-maker** firm – for example, the market leader, or a business having a local or other monopoly – can set the market price which others will follow, but it will still need to take account of competitors' prices if their pricing policies start affecting its sales and market position.

> **EXAMINER'S TOP TIP**
> In your answers about price, you may need to state that most firms use both cost-based and market-based information to make pricing decisions.

Pricing strategy £ $ €

- A business using a **skimming** (or **creaming**) strategy sets a high price for a new, innovative product. In this way it hopes to **maximise profits** in the short term, until competitors enter the market with alternatives that – as a result of this competition – will force prices down. The original skimming price is possible because there are no alternatives to the product, its **scarcity value** boosting its appeal and its demand.
- A business may also use a **penetration** strategy with a new product (and this strategy can also be applied to existing products). The strategy is one of **lower prices**, and lower profit margins. The purpose of penetration pricing is to **increase market share** at the expense of competitors. It is associated with:
  - high-volume, long life and price-sensitive products
  - firms that can benefit from economies of scale, and which have a competitive cost advantage.
- Skimming and penetration strategies may be further refined, by considering the **psychological** influence of the prices set. The price may be adjusted either in **amount** (for example, from £10.00 to £9.95 because it 'looks cheaper') or due to the **image** or other features of the product – consumers expect products with an 'exclusive' image to carry an 'exclusive' price.
- **Predator pricing** shares some of the characteristics of penetration pricing in that it is market-based, occurs when a firm sets its prices deliberately below those of competitors, and applies to existing products. However, it is a more aggressive move, to take control of the market by deliberately undercutting a rival's prices in an attempt to drive the rival out of the market. One way a business can afford the likely short-term losses associated with this strategy – because the low price it sets may be below its product cost – is through **cross-subsidy**, using profits made by another product in its portfolio.
- A firm may also use **pricing tactics**, a shorter-term approach to pricing. An example is **loss leaders**, where price is used as a form of sales promotion. This is a popular tactic with supermarkets, who set below-cost prices on certain items, and use this to tempt customers into the store in the hope that other products – priced above cost – will also be bought on the same shopping trip.

> **EXAMINER'S TOP TIP**
> Economics (price mechanism), Accounts (cost and revenue) and Marketing (market prices) all have an influence on pricing strategy.

Quick test

1 State one internal and one external influence on the price set by a firm.
2 Name two forms of cost-based approaches to pricing.
3 Identify the main weakness associated with a cost-based pricing approach.
4 Outline the difference between a skimming and a penetration price strategy.

1. internal: e.g. costs incurred, overall objectives; external: e.g. competitors' prices, nature of the market 2. cost-plus pricing; contribution pricing 3. There is a risk that market-based information will be ignored when setting prices. 4. skimming: high price initially set for an innovative new product in the market; penetration: low price set in an attempt to increase market share

Elasticity of demand

Elasticity

- The level of demand for products is influenced by many factors. Price, and the level of consumer income, are two important influences on how demand for products changes over time.
- Calculating a product's <u>elasticity of demand</u> is a measure of the change in its demand, or quantity demanded. Elasticity of demand is influenced by changes in:

Price OR **Income**

Price elasticity of demand (PED)

- Price is normally the most important short-term influence on the quantity demanded. PED measures how responsive the product is to changes in its price, helping explain the effect that a change in price will have on the product's sales. It assesses <u>movements along the demand curve</u>, rather than shifts in the demand curve.
- PED can be calculated:

$$\text{Price elasticity (PED)} = \frac{\text{Percentage change in quantity demanded}}{\text{Percentage change in price}}$$

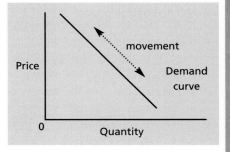

- If the price of the product increases from £5 to £6, and quantity demanded falls from 500 to 450 a month, PED = 10/20 = 0.5. Demand is <u>price-elastic</u> when PED is greater than 1 (the calculation gives a negative '−0.5 ' answer, and the minus sign is often ignored), and <u>price-inelastic</u> when PED is below 1.
- In this case, PED is below 1, so the supplier knows that a change in price will cause a less than proportionate change in quantity demanded: the product is <u>price-insensitive</u>. If PED had been above 1, the product would be <u>price-sensitive</u>, the quantity demanded being heavily influenced by price changes.
- Here, because the product is price inelastic, the increase in its price has resulted in total monthly revenue increasing from £2 500 (£5 × 500) to £2 700 (£6 × 450).
- If PED = 1, the product is said to have <u>unitary elasticity</u>, since the percentage change in quantity demanded equals the percentage change in price.

For the supplier

Where the price is *inelastic* (PED < 1)		Where the price is *elastic* (PED > 1)	
Price increases	**Price falls**	**Price increases**	**Price falls**
↓	↓	↓	↓
Revenue increases	**Revenue falls**	**Revenue falls**	**Revenue increases**
because the quantity demanded has risen or fallen by a **lower** percentage than the price change		because the quantity demanded has risen or fallen by a **higher** percentage than the price change	

Price elasticity and the supplier

- Some products are far more price-sensitive than others. There are a number of influences on the PED of a product. These include:
  - the availability of <u>substitutes</u> – a product that has a close substitute (for example, butter and margarine) tends to have a price-elastic demand since consumers can easily switch between the products
  - its <u>price</u> – less expensive products often have a price-inelastic demand because changes in price have little effect on consumers' pockets
  - <u>addiction</u> – addictive products such as tobacco have a price-inelastic demand since the decision to buy is not based on rational price information.

EXAMINER'S TOP TIP

A change in demand is different to a change in the quantity demanded.

Using the information

- Firms can use PED information to:
  - plan their pricing strategy – PED data can be used with information about costs to help decide on prices to charge
  - forecast their sales – different forecasts can be prepared for a range of prices, if PED is known.
- A business may try to make its product <u>more price-inelastic</u> because this would allow it to increase profits (in the short term) by simply increasing the product's price. It may have some success in increasing price inelasticity through <u>differentiating</u> the product to a greater extent or highlighting its <u>USP</u> in order to charge a higher price, or by establishing more of a <u>monopoly</u> position in the market to reduce the effect of a competitor's pricing policy on the demand for its product.

EXAMINER'S TOP TIP
Practise calculating PED and IED by using your own figures.

Income elasticity of demand (IED)

- IED measures how responsive demand for the product is as consumer income changes. IED can be linked to <u>changes in the demand curve</u>, since it is based on changes in real disposable income.
- IED can be calculated:

$$\text{Income elasticity (IED)} = \frac{\text{Percentage change in quantity demanded}}{\text{Percentage change in real income}}$$

- (Real income refers to income after inflation has been taken into account.) Demand is <u>income-elastic</u> when IED is greater than 1, and <u>income-inelastic</u> when IED is less than 1.
- For example, a 5 % rise in consumer real incomes might result in consumers spending 10 % more on going to the cinema. In this case, going to the cinema would be regarded as being <u>income-elastic</u>.
- IED is mainly influenced by the <u>type of product</u> being bought:
  - <u>luxuries</u> and <u>non-necessities</u> are normally income-elastic, because the demand for these goods increases at a faster rate than the increase in real income
  - <u>necessities</u> or <u>basic</u> products, such as bread and milk, are normally income-inelastic, since a change in income has little effect on demand.
- <u>Inferior</u> goods may have a negative income elasticity because, as they become better off, consumers tend to buy fewer of, or spend less on, these items.

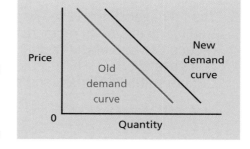

Quick test

1 State the calculation for:

  a PED

  b IED.

2 Outline one influence on the PED of a product.

3 State one way that a business might use information about the price elasticity of its products.

4 What are 'real incomes'?

1. a) % change in quantity demanded divided by % change in price b) % change in real incomes divided by % change in real income 2. e. g. availability of substitutes, price, addiction 3. e.g. in forecasting sales (a range of forecasts could be prepared using PED information), in planning pricing strategy 4. Incomes that are adjusted for inflation

43

Exam-style questions Use the questions to test your progress. Check your answers on pages 92–95.

Exam-style questions

Marketing

1   TieBuy Ltd is a small company that makes and sells a range of men's ties. Outline **two** advantages and **two** disadvantages to TieBuy Ltd from operating in a niche market.   [4]

   ....

   ....

   ....

2   Outline and justify **one** appropriate way of segmenting the market for these products:
   a   a new private health club   [2]

   ....

   ....

   b   a new range of A-level textbooks   [2]

   ....

   ....

   c   a brand of breakfast cereals.   [2]

   ....

   ....

3   The manager of the Hideaway Hotel, based in a medium-sized town, is disappointed with the trading results of its restaurant, which is open to non-residents. As a result, she is planning to reduce the size of the restaurant and convert part of it to a gym, for use by both guests and non-guests.
   Outline suitable primary and secondary research that the manager could undertake.   [5]

   ....

   ....

   ....

   ....

4   Hughes Ltd makes and sells a small range of biscuits and cereal bars. These products are sold nationally, but the company has not been able to sell them to the large national retailers. As a result, the biscuits and bars are sold in small independent retail outlets throughout the UK.
   The current product portfolio for Hughes Ltd's biscuits and cereal bars consists of:
   • **Bran Biscuit**, a recently introduced biscuit 'with added bran for healthy digestion', whose sales have now started to increase quickly
   • **Chunky Chews**, a well-established market leading cereal bar with high sales and 'added chocolate chunks'
   • **Dunk'em Delights**, once the company's best-selling biscuit but now marketed at a 'value for money' price since its sales started to fall last year
   • **Fruitee Fig Bars**, a fruit and fig cereal bar just launched onto the market (the company hopes to gain a 2% market share in the first year, and is pricing this product accordingly)
   • **Minty Munchies**, a chocolate-coated, mint-flavoured biscuit that started to lose sales, but is now selling as well as ever (it is thought) as a result of re-naming and package re-design.

   a   What is meant by 'product portfolio'?   [1]

   ....

b Classify each of Hughes Ltd's products using the product life-cycle. Give a reason for your classifications. [4]

....

....

....

....

....

c Explain the new-product development stages that Hughes Ltd would have gone through to produce and market Fruitee Fig Bars. [6]

....

....

....

....

d Give **one** example of a product-extension strategy used by Hughes Ltd. [1]

....

e Suggest and justify **one** appropriate channel of distribution for Hughes Ltd's products. [3]

....

....

f Select and justify a pricing strategy for the Fruitee Fig Bars. [2]

....

....

5 Select **one** suitable advertising medium for each of the following. Select a different medium in each case, and justify your selection.

a A used car being sold privately [2]

....

b a new game, based on a recent successful movie, for a major games console [2]

....

c a new store being opened in an out-of-town shopping centre. [2]

....

6 The managers of a business have cut the price of its product by 5% from £10.00. As a result, the weekly number bought has increased from 10 000 to 11 000 units.

a) Calculate the price elasticity of demand. [2]

....

b State whether the product is price-elastic or price-inelastic. [1]

....

c State, using appropriate calculations, whether the managers were justified in reducing the product's price. [4]

....

....

Total: /45

Types of cost

Fixed and variable

- Fixed and variable costs refer to <u>cost behaviour</u>: how costs behave (change) as output changes.
- This classification is important for <u>break-even analysis</u>, and helps managers <u>control</u> costs.

<u>Fixed costs</u>
– do not vary with output
– have business rent and rates as typical examples

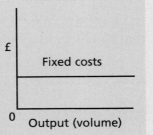

<u>Variable costs</u>
– vary <u>directly</u> with output
– have raw materials and piecework wages as typical examples.

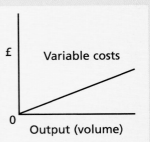

- In practice, fixed costs will change over time: for example, business rates or office staff salaries may increase during the financial year.
- Variable costs may not change exactly as output changes: examples include receiving discounts for prompt payment (which reduces the unit cost of the materials bought) or paying overtime rates to manufacturing labour (increasing the average variable cost per hour).

<u>Semi-variable costs</u> may be found.

- These costs, also known as <u>semi-fixed</u>, have both a fixed and a variable element.
- Power is a popular example: e.g. electricity charges may have a fixed ('standing') element, plus an amount per kilowatt used. Another example is the 'landline' telephone, which often has a fixed line-rental payable whether or not any calls are made.

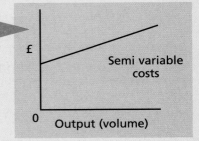

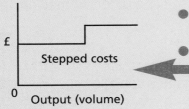

- <u>Stepped costs</u> may also exist. These (fixed) costs change as output changes.
- An example is business rent, where at some stage an increase in a firm's output forces it to rent additional premises for work or storage purposes.

<u>Total costs</u> consist of the total fixed costs plus the total variable costs.

- The firm can calculate <u>average total costs</u>, which are likely to fall as output increases.
- The reason for this is that <u>the same total for fixed costs is spread over an increasing output</u>. As a result, the fixed costs per unit fall, reducing the <u>average total costs</u> as shown below.

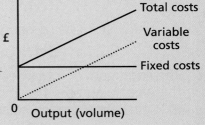

Output (units)	Fixed costs £	Variable costs £	Total costs £	Average total costs £
100	1 200	100	1 300	13
200	1 200	200	1 400	7
300	1 200	300	1 500	5
400	1 200	400	1 600	4

EXAMINER'S TOP TIP
The practical difficulties of identifying costs as truly fixed or variable are important limitations of break-even analysis.

Direct and indirect costs

- This classification is important for <u>absorption costing</u>, a costing method that 'absorbs' the various costs into production cost for the firm's products. It also gives information that can be used for <u>product pricing</u> (e.g. 'cost plus' pricing) and <u>stock valuation</u>.
- <u>Direct costs</u> are directly related to the production of particular products, and can be <u>allocated</u> to a particular cost or profit centre.
- Examples of direct costs include raw materials and production wages.

- <u>Indirect costs</u> are also known as '<u>overheads</u>', and are <u>not</u> directly attributable to products. They must therefore be <u>apportioned</u> (shared out).
- How indirect costs are apportioned will affect the individual costs of the firm's products, and therefore decisions about these products.
- Examples of overheads include factory and office rent and rates, selling expenses, administration expenses.

Costs, revenue and profit

- Sales revenue = number sold × unit price.
- Prices vary in practice: for example, special offers, and when selling in home and overseas markets. Some firms sell high-priced products with high profit margins (e.g. some jewellery); other businesses such as mass-market retailers like Asda sell large volumes with low profit margins.
- The interaction between these is <u>cost–volume–profit</u> (CVP) analysis.
- <u>Profit</u> is important because it:
  - is a reward to entrepreneurs for risk-taking
  - encourages investment in companies by shareholders.
  - can be used to measure the success of a business
  - leads to banks and other lenders supporting the firm
- Profit is either 'saved' by the business by being reinvested (and through not being spent, it preserves the business's cash) or 'spent', as either enforced (business taxes are based on profits) or voluntary spending (e.g. dividends).
- Profit can be classified as:
  - <u>gross</u> profit, the difference between sales revenue and the cost of these sales, and <u>net</u> profit, (the gross profit less all other expenses)
  - <u>operating</u> profit (gross profit less production-based costs), <u>profit before tax</u>, and <u>profit after tax</u>.

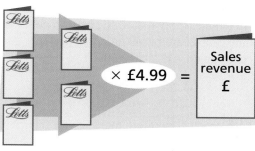

EXAMINER'S TOP TIP

Falling average total costs is a good example of economies of scale.

Quick Test

1 *Choosing one option from each bullet point below, classify the various costs listed below under their most likely heading:*
- *fixed, variable or semi-variable*
- *direct or indirect.*

a Office manager's salary; b sales force (100% commission); c materials used to make the product; d advertising costs; e electricity; f interest paid; g machine operator's wages.

2 *Outline how a company 'spends' or 'saves' its profits.*

3 *A company has produced these figures: total fixed costs £1 850; total variable costs £430; total revenue £4 300. Calculate the profit or loss.*

4 *A firm's product sells for £18.50; its unit variable costs are £7.40 and its total fixed costs are £40 000. It has made and sold 5 000 products. Calculate the total profit or loss.*

£92 500; total variable costs 5 000 × £7.40 = £37 000 so total costs are £77 000 and profit is £15 500
direct. 2. 'spends' in the form of dividends or taxes; 'saves' through reinvestment 3. £2020 profit 4. total revenue 5 000 × £18.50 =
1. a) fixed, indirect. b) variable. c) variable, direct. d) fixed, indirect. e) semi-variable, indirect. f) fixed, indirect. g) variable,

Break-even analysis

Fixed and variable costs

- The purpose of break-even analysis is to establish the point at which the business is making neither a profit nor a loss: this is the output at which it breaks even because <u>total revenue = total costs.</u>
- Break-even analysis can be used to:

explore the effect of proposed price changes on profits	set sales and production targets	study how changing fixed and variable costs affect profit levels.

Calculating break-even

- We already know that fixed costs do not change as output changes, whereas variable costs will change.
- Calculations are based on <u>contribution</u>. Every product has a variable cost and a selling price. A product's unit contribution is calculated by:

$$\text{Unit contribution} = \text{selling price} - \text{unit variable cost}$$

- Each product therefore makes a 'contribution' towards meeting the total fixed costs. When enough of these individual contributions are made, the firm's fixed costs will be covered and it will be at its break-even point. The break-even calculation formula is therefore:

$$\text{Break-even} = \frac{\text{Total fixed costs}}{\text{Unit contribution}}$$

- If, therefore, a firm has fixed costs totalling £6 000, variable costs of £1.00 per unit, and a unit selling price of £2.50:
  - unit contribution = £2.50 – £1.00 = £1.50
  - break-even is £6 000/£1.50 = 4 000 units.
- The <u>break-even revenue</u> can be calculated (break-even output × selling price):
  - 4 000 × £2.50 = £10 000.

- These calculations can easily be checked:
  - total revenue = £10 000 (as above)
  - total costs = £10 000 (fixed £6 000 + variable £4 000 [4 000 × £1.00]).

- Contribution analysis can also be used to calculate profit or loss once the break-even point is known.
  - Profit = contribution × number of units above the break-even point
  - Loss = contribution × number of units below the break-even point.

- In the above example, if the firm made and sold 6 000 units, it makes a profit of £3 000 (2 000 units above break-even × £1.50 contribution).
- Had this firm made and sold only 3 800 units, its loss would have been £300 (£200 units below break-even × £1.50).
- The <u>margin of safety</u> for a firm is shown by the amount of output and sales above the break-even point. This shows by how much production and sales can fall before the firm moves from profit into loss.
  - For the above firm, making and selling 6 000 units, its margin of safety is 2 000 units (6 000 made and sold – 4 000 break-even).

EXAMINER'S TOP TIP
If asked to draw a break-even chart, remember that you can probably check its accuracy by also calculating the break-even point.

Graphical display

- The sales revenue line is plotted from the zero output point; the fixed cost line is plotted; the total cost line, starting where the fixed cost line meets the vertical axis, is plotted.
- Break-even is where the total revenue and total cost lines intersect.
- Here is the break-even chart constructed using the figures we met on the last page.

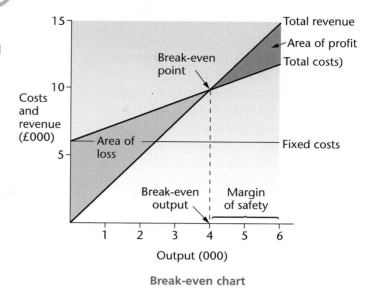

Break-even chart

> **EXAMINER'S TOP TIP**
> When drawing your break-even chart, the '£ costs and revenue' scale normally reaches the value of the maximum total revenue.

Limitations of break-even analysis

- In practice, break-even analysis may be of limited use.
- The break-even calculations apply to a single product, or to a set 'mix' of products. Firms producing and selling varying amounts of different products therefore find it difficult to produce meaningful break-even analysis.
- Not all costs are easily classified as fixed or variable, which is a fundamental requirement for break-even analysis.
- There is an assumption that selling prices and unit variable costs remain the same regardless of output, which is often unrealistic. Selling prices may be altered, e.g. by a retailer at 'August sales' time, and unit variable costs will also vary, e.g. as a result of receiving discounts when buying in bulk.
- Fixed costs may also change over time, which affects the accuracy of break-even calculations.
- Production and sales are assumed to be same, which is not likely to be so in reality.

Quick test

1. State three purposes of carrying out break-even analysis.
2. Explain and illustrate the terms:
   a contribution
   b margin of safety.
3. Calculate the break-even point for a firm that has total fixed costs of £440 000, unit variable costs of £6.00, and a selling price of £11.50.
4. If the above firm makes and sells 75 000 products, calculate its profit or loss and its margin of safety.
5. Identify three limitations of using break-even analysis.

1. to assess how changes in price may affect selling price and variable cost, e.g. selling price £5.00, variable cost £3.00, contribution = £2.00 b) margin of safety: the amount of production/sales over and above the break-even point, e.g. break-even output 5 000, number made and sold 8 000, margin of safety 3 000 3. £440 000/(£11.50 − £6.00) = 80 000 units: break-even revenue of £920 000 (80 000 × £11.50) 4. It sells 5 000 units (80 000 − 75 000) below break-even, so a loss of 5 000 × £5.50 contribution = £27 500. There is no margin of safety since the firm does not reach its break-even point. 5. fixed costs may vary over time; selling prices may change over a range of output; the firm may make and sell a number of different products, and break-even analysis is best suited to a single product

Cash-flow management

- 'Cash flow' and 'profit' are two distinct areas of finance. Cash flow indicates the movement of cash into and out of a business. Profit is a calculation of by how much the business's revenue (income) exceeds its expenses.

- There are various reasons why a firm's cash flow will be different from its profit. The accrual concept in financial accounting makes a business match its expenses and revenues to the relevant accounting period – when cash is received or paid is not relevant. For example, sales made on credit this year that are paid for next year, affect this year's profits although the cash received affects next year's cash balance.

- Other examples include:

| items for which cash is paid that do not affect profits – e.g. buying fixed assets reduces cash but has no effect on profits | receipts of cash that have nothing to do with profits – e.g. cash received from a loan or a share issue | non-cash expenses that reduce profits but do not affect cash – e.g. depreciation. |

- The profit figure is a key element in assessing a firm's profitability – the measure of its success established by comparing its profits to a relevant figure such as the capital it employs.

- Cash is a key element in assessing a firm's liquidity – its ability to meet its debts as they fall due for payment.

- A firm's profitability is more important in the long run, because in the short run it can survive without profits, although it cannot survive long without having sufficient cash to pay its debts.

- Since cash flow is so important to a firm and to the assessment of its prospects, firms produce cash-flow forecasts and cash-flow statements:

  - a cash-flow forecast is produced in order to anticipate future cash flows in and out of the firm (similar to a cash budget)

  - a cash-flow statement must be produced by companies and published along with the other key financial statements such as the profit and loss account and the balance sheet, as a record and analysis of its cash flows in and out during the last financial year.

Cash-flow statement	£000
Cash flows from profits	XXX
Interest and dividends	XXX
Capital expenditure	XXX
Long-term financing	XXX
Net movement of cash	XXX

Constructing the cash-flow forecast

- Cash-flow forecasts are used to assess cash needs. Constructing the forecast allows the firm to manage its cash resources more efficiently. It can check:
  - the timing and amount of its cash inflows
  - the timing and amount of its cash outflows
  - its forecast cash flow with the actual cash flow, and explore reasons for any differences.

EXAMINER'S TOP TIP

Remember that a business can have too much (surplus) cash as well as too little.

How to construct a cash-flow forcast

At the end of December a firm has £6 000 cash and debtors of £75 000; creditors (credit suppliers) are £40 000, and it owes £20 000 in tax, to be paid in March. It gives its debtors a month's credit, and it receives one month's credit from its creditors. Each month, overheads are £20 000 and wages are £25 000, and are paid in the same month. Forecast sales and purchases (all on credit) are (£000):

	Jan	Feb	Mar
Sales	100	125	105
Purchases	50	60	60

- The cash-flow forecast is shown in the table.

- This cash-flow forecast has therefore identified a potential cash shortage in January, and the firm will need to take appropriate action such as arranging a temporary overdraft with its bank.

EXAMINER'S TOP TIP
We must recognise that the cash-flow forecast is likely to be inaccurate, with actual receipts and payments differing from those in the forecast.

	January (£000)	February (£000)	March (£000)
Receipts (inflows)			
Cash from debtors	75	100	125
Total receipts	75	100	125
Payments (outflows)			
Cash paid to suppliers	40	50	60
Overheads	20	20	20
Wages	25	25	25
Tax			20
Total payments	85	95	125
Net cash flow	(10)	5	0
Opening balance	6	(4)	1
Closing balance	(4)	1	1

Action based on the cash-flow forecast

- If the forecast indicates that cash inflows need to be improved, the firm's managers have several strategies open to them:
  - 'debtor days' and 'creditor days' ratios can be calculated to indicate the speed of receipts and payments in an attempt to quicken inflows and slow down outflows
  - debts can be factored – sold to a factoring (debt-collecting) agent, at the cost of a percentage of the total debt, to obtain cash early

- instead of paying cash for new fixed assets, spending may be cut by acquiring them through leasing to avoid major outlays of cash
- sale and leaseback of assets already owned could gain cash for the business
- other spending may be delayed
- short-term and long-term borrowing can be arranged.

Quick test

1 Give one example of how the amounts of profit and cash made may differ in a financial year.
2 Outline the difference between: a cash flow and liquidity b profit and profitability.
3 What is the difference between a cash-flow forecast and a cash-flow statement?
4 How does cash-flow forecasting aid the survival of a firm?

1. Buying machinery and paying cash will reduce the firm's cash balance but not directly affect its profit. Receiving cash from issues of shares increases the cash balance but does not affect profits. Depreciation reduces profits but is a non-cash expense, so cash in unaffected. 2. a) Cash flow is concerned with cash inflows and outflows; liquidity indicates the ability of a firm to meet its short-term cash debts. b) Profit is the excess of income over expenditure; profitability compares the amount of profit to some other measure to indicate the level of success for the firm. 3. The forecast looks ahead to expected movements of cash; the statement looks back by analysing past movements of cash. 4. It can indicate the likely future liquidity of the firm (enabling it to anticipate cash shortages and therefore plan to overcome them) and also any cash surpluses for possible investment.

Sources of finance

Selecting the source

- The long-term funds and other sources of finance used by a business are summarised in its <u>balance sheet</u>, which shows its financial position at a particular point in time.
- The balance sheet of NAM Ltd (below) illustrates the main sources of funds typically used by a company:

short-term funding through:
- using trade credit, shown as Creditors under the Current Liabilities he
ading

long-term investment by the owners:
- share capital in the case of companies
- the undistributed profits in the Profit & Loss Reserve balance

other external borrowing, through loans from banks and other lenders.

Balance Sheet of NAM Ltd as at 31 December:		
	£000	£000
Fixed assets (net book value)		450
Current assets	220	
Current liabilities	140	
Net current assets (working capital)		80
Net assets		530
Share capital		250
Reserves (profit and loss account)		80
Shareholder's equity		330
Long term loan		200
		530

- It is important to ensure the <u>source is appropriate for the use</u> to which the finance will be put.
- Short-term projects, which normally run for less than a year, will have different funding requirements to medium-term (between 1 and 5 years) and long-term (over 5 years) projects.

Short term ⟺	Medium term ⟺	Long term
(up to one year)	(between one and five years)	(over five years)
Overdrafts	Credit sale/hire purchase	Share capital
Trade credit	Leasing	Retained profits
Factoring		Loans

<u>form</u> of the business – for example, sole traders and partnerships cannot issue share capital, and private limited companies cannot ask the general public to subscribe in their share capital

<u>stability</u> of the business – influences include whether it:
- is new or established
- operates in an expanding or contracting market
- faces fierce competition

<u>economy</u> – e.g. whether the economy overall is booming or in a period of decline

Other influences on the source of funds

<u>track record</u> of the business – e.g. its profit performance in recent years

EXAMINER'S TOP TIP
Make sure that any source you recommend for a particular situation is relevant to that situation.

Internal sources

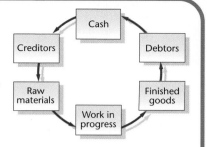

The operating cycle

- The short-term internal sources of funds are generated from the business's <u>working capital</u>. This is the difference between its <u>current assets</u> and its <u>current liabilities</u>.
- Stock, debtors (credit customers) and cash are the main current assets, representing actual or 'near' cash. Creditors, bank overdraft, and tax owing are the main current liabilities, which represent short-term debts owed by the business. Any surplus of current assets indicates the business is able to meet its short-term debts through turning stock and debtors into cash.
- The business may use <u>trade credit</u> as a source of finance, mainly through extending the credit period it takes from its suppliers. Doing so, however, can increase its costs because the business can no longer take up the favourable discount terms being offered, and may also lead to problems if suppliers withdraw their offer of credit due to slow payment.
- The business can also sell any <u>surplus fixed assets</u> such as machinery and vehicles, which will generate cash in the short term.
- <u>Retained profit</u> is a longer-term source of finance, whereby the firm preserves its cash through retaining its profits rather than paying them in the form of dividends: if this policy is over-used, shareholders may become dissatisfied, and the share price could be affected.

> **EXAMINER'S TOP TIP**
> Make sure that any source you recommend for a particular situation is relevant to that situation.

> **EXAMINER'S TOP TIP**
> Sources of funds can be classified according to whether they are **internal** to the firm or from an **external** provider, and by the length of project

External sources

- An important short-term source of funds is the <u>bank overdraft</u>. This gives the business flexibility in terms of how much is borrowed, the cost of the borrowing being based on the amount overdrawn from its bank account.
- Debt <u>factoring</u> is an alternative short-term external source, where the business sells its debts to a factoring company and in return receives an immediate payment of most of the debt.
- <u>Leasing</u> is an important source of finance, with the firm being able to obtain and use the relevant fixed asset without having to buy it outright. This preserves its cash at the start of the arrangement, although the firm is now committed to making regular payments as long at it continues to lease the asset.
- <u>Credit sale</u> and <u>hire purchase</u> are examples of medium- and long-term sources available to firms. These methods allow firms to spread the cost of their capital expenditure over a long period of time.
- Long-term sources include <u>loans</u> and the issue of <u>share capital</u> (for companies). Loans may be in the form of a <u>debenture</u>, which may be secured against a particular asset in the firm: if the firm cannot meet its payments, the lender can obtain that asset in return for non-payment.

	Loan capital	Share capital
Provided by:	lenders	owners
Effect on control:	no direct effect on the firm	direct effect on the firm
Payment of:	interest	dividends
Payment taken from:	gross (untaxed) profit	net (taxed) profit
Failure to pay:	may close the firm down	leads to dissatisfied shareholders

Quick test

1 **List three sources of funds used by a company.**

2 **Define the term 'working capital'.**

3 **What is 'trade credit'?**

4 **List two sources of finance that are normally classified as:**
   a **short term**   b **medium term**   c **long term.**

5 **State two ways that loan capital differs from share capital.**

1. e.g. share capital, reserves, trade credit, loan, factoring debts, overdraft. 2. the difference between a firm's current assets and its current liabilities 3. the use of delayed payments to creditors to help finance purchases of stock 4. a) overdrafts, trade credit, factoring b) credit sale, hire purchase, leasing c) share capital, retained profits, loans 5. e.g. loan capital: interest is paid, rather than dividends (share capital); the lenders of loan capital have no direct say in the business, unlike shareholders

Budgeting

- **A budget is a <u>financial plan for a given period</u>. By setting budgets, therefore, firms <u>plan</u> their activities – e.g. planning sales, and for cash movements such as capital expenditure purchases. Firms also:**
  - <u>co-ordinate</u> their activities – for example, having a <u>master budget</u> that is constructed from the other budgets encourages different business functions and departments to work closely together
  - <u>control</u> their activities – by comparing the budgeted figures (set in advance) with the actual results when the given time period has elapsed
  - <u>communicate</u> their activities – by getting all staff involved in constructing the budgets for which they will be fully or partly responsible.
- **Budgets also <u>motivate</u> staff, both through getting them involved in preparation and by setting targets for them to achieve.**

Setting budgets

- Stages in setting budgets include:

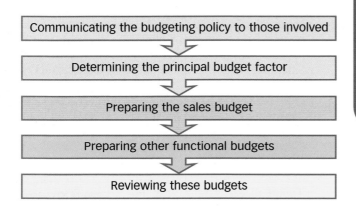

Zero budgeting

- A <u>zero-base</u> budgeting system is when managers have their budgets initially set at zero.
- The advantage of this approach is that managers have to fully justify all expenditure for which they are responsible. Zero budgeting therefore makes managers <u>establish priorities</u>, and link their plans to the key objectives of the firm.

- Budgets are set for a given period. The length of this period depends on factors such as the type of business – e.g. firms in fashion-based industries such as clothing work on shorter budget periods than those based in industries where fashions are less important.
- Budgeting is a formal process. A **<u>budget committee</u>** is established to oversee the construction and co-ordination of all the firm's budgets, and a **<u>budget manual</u>** is created to record the various procedures to be followed.
- The **<u>principal budget factor</u>**, also known as the 'key' or 'limiting' factor, has to be recognised and accounted for in the budgets. This is the item that limits the firm's activities. Examples of commonly used principal budget factors are the:

level of <u>demand</u> for the firm's products	availability of <u>suitably skilled labour</u> in the firm	volume of <u>materials</u> that the firm can buy and use	availability of any <u>specialist machinery</u> that is required	amount of <u>space</u> available for production.

- Budgets are set for the key functions of the firm. The first budget normally set is the <u>sales budget</u>, because the level of sales demand is normally the principal budget factor. In setting the sales budget, sales units and value are calculated, using a combination of:
  - previous sales figures
  - current market research and conditions
  - an estimate of the level of competition.

EXAMINER'S TOP TIP
There is a key difference between Budgeting (a planning and coordination focus) and Budgetary Control (a control focus).

The main budgets

- The <u>production</u> budget is based on the sales budget. Numbers to be made are calculated on the basis of:
  - how many are to be sold
  - stock levels
  - the time lag between manufacture and sale.
- From the production budget, other budgets, e.g. for <u>material purchases</u> and <u>direct labour</u>, will be calculated.
- The <u>cash</u> budget will be constructed from information contained in the above and other (e.g. capital expenditure) budgets. It summarises cash inflows and outflows.

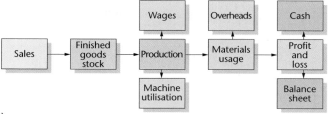

The main budgets

- Once the various functional budgets are completed, the <u>budgeted profit and loss account</u> and the <u>budgeted balance sheet</u> can be prepared. These 'final accounts' budgets set overall targets for the firm to achieve, such as the total profit expected to be made.

Difficulties of budgeting

- Budgets are difficult to set accurately in practice. Problems include using information that may be:
  - <u>incomplete</u>   • <u>inaccurate</u>   • <u>out of date</u>.
- Because budgets can be difficult to set, and since they involve targets being set, there can be a temptation to set targets that are <u>too easily achieved</u>.
- There is also a tendency to look for simple but often inaccurate solutions, such as the 'last year's figures plus a percentage for inflation' approach, which lacks the justifications required in a zero-budgeting approach.

EXAMINER'S TOP TIP
Remember the 'three Cs' of budgeting – <u>C</u>ontrol, <u>C</u>o-ordinate and <u>C</u>ommunicate – as well as 'PM' (<u>P</u>lan and <u>M</u>otivate).

Budgetary control

- Once budgets have been planned and are operating, it becomes possible to compare the <u>actual</u> results against the results <u>expected</u> in the budget.
- Budgetary control can be operated in most types of organisation, trading and non-trading. It is also widely used in both the private sector and the public sector. Budgetary control may be linked with a <u>standard costing</u> system.

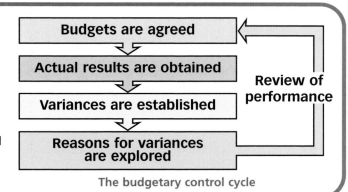

The budgetary control cycle

Quick test

1 **Place these budgets in their typical order of construction: production, sales, labour, profit & loss, cash.**

2 **a Give two alternative names for 'principal budget factor'.**

   b State three examples of a principal budget factor.

3 **Suggest two influences on the construction of a production budget.**

4 **What base does a 'zero budget' start from?**

5 **Give one advantage associated with zero budgeting.**

1. sales, production, labour, cash, profit & loss.   2. a) limiting, or key   b) demand for the product, skilled labour, materials, specialist machinery, space available for production   3. e.g. the level of budgeted sales, the number of finished goods in stock, time lag between manufacture and sales.   4. zero   5. Managers must justify any item in their budget.

55

Interpreting variances

EXAMINER'S TOP TIP

Don't confuse <u>management by exception</u> with management by <u>objectives</u>.

- <u>Control</u> takes place through management by exception. This control technique is based on the comparison of actual against expected (budget). The difference between the budgeted and actual performance is known as a <u>variance</u>.
- Some variances will be due to factors that are under the control of a manager. Other variances may arise from factors outside the manager's control. For example:
  - the product's selling price is likely to be controllable by the firm, so the sales manager could be held responsible for variances arising from this
  - abour costs may
  be under the control of the firm,
  although a nationally agreed pay rise is outside its control
  - the price paid for, and quality of, materials used are likely to be under a manager's control

  - production overheads such as rent are probably not controllable (in the short term)
  - selling costs such as advertising, and administration costs, are likely to be controllable by managers.
- <u>Managers can only be held responsible for variances they can control.</u>

Types of variance

- Variances are either:
  - <u>favourable</u> – e.g. where the amount paid for a particular cost such as raw materials is below the budgeted cost, or where actual sales revenue is above the budgeted figure
  - <u>adverse</u> (unfavourable) – e.g. where the actual sales revenue is below the budgeted revenue, or when the actual cost of wages paid is above budget.

- For example, here is the budget summary for a firm. Covering the trading period January–June, the various budgets are set before this period starts. The summary shows a <u>revenue</u> budget (sales), and a series of <u>cost</u> budgets. The overall budgeted profit is calculated by deducting the expected total costs from the expected sales revenue.

- Once this period is over, the firm's **actual performance** can be compared with the budget.
- Now that both the budgeted and actual figures are known, each variance can be calculated.

Note that, if actual <u>revenue</u> is above budgeted there will be a favourable ('good') variance, whereas if actual <u>costs</u> are above budget the variance will be adverse ('bad').

Budget summary, January–June	
	(£) Budget (£)
Sales revenue	265 000
Costs:	
labour	60 000
materials	42 000
production overheads	15 500
selling costs	12 500
administration costs	20 000
Total costs:	**150 000**
Profit (sales less costs)	115 000

Comparison of actual against budget, January–June			
	(£) Budget (£)		(£) Actual (£)
Sales revenue	265 000		255 000
Costs:			
labour	60 000		55 250
materials	42 000		45 100
production overheads	15 500		16 200
selling costs	12 500		12 150
administration costs	20 000		22 300
Total costs:	**150 000**		**151 000**
Profit (sales less costs)	115 000		104 000

Types of variance continued

EXAMINER'S TOP TIP

After calculating a variance, remember to state whether it is favourable or adverse.

- Sales: Actual revenue is below that budgeted, so the variance is adverse.
- Costs: Labour and selling costs are below those budgeted, producing favourable variances; materials, production overheads and administrative costs are all above budget, producing adverse variances.
- The overall profit variance of £11 000 adverse is therefore made up of all adverse variances, totalling £16 100, less all favourable variances, which total £5 100.

Variance calculations						
	(£)	Budget (£)	(£)	Actual (£)	(£) Variance	(£)
					Favourable	Adverse
Sales revenue		265 000		255 000		10 000
Costs:						
labour	60 000		55 250		4 750	
materials	42 000		45 100			3 100
production overheads	15 500		16 200			700
selling costs	12 500		12 150		350	
administration costs	20 000		22 300			2 300
Total costs:		150 000		151 000		
Profit (sales less costs)		115 000		104 000		
Total variances					5 100	16 100
Profit (sales less costs)		115 000		104 000		11 000

Reasons for variances

- There may be several reasons behind each variance. Possible reasons for the above variances are given below.
  - **Sales**: Fewer units may have been sold, or sold at a lower price than that budgeted for.
  - **Labour**: A cheaper grade of labour may have been used, or employees may have worked more efficiently than expected.
  - **Materials**: More materials were used than expected, or they cost more than planned.
  - **Production overheads**: Factory costs such as rent may have been higher than expected.
  - **Selling costs**: Less was spent on selling than planned, perhaps because there were fewer sold.
  - **Administration costs**: These were higher than expected, perhaps due to a pay rise for office staff that was higher than that budgeted for.
- In practice, the budget may need to be **flexed** if it is based on sales or output figures that are different to those that actually occur. As an example, it would be incorrect to compare budgeted figures based on making and selling 25 000 units if the actual number sold was – and therefore actual costs and revenues were based on – 30 000.

Quick test

1 **State the variances in the following situations:**

a **actual sales £300 000 compared with budgeted sales £285 000**

b **budgeted materials £27 500, actual cost paid £30 000**

c **production overheads £4 000 actual, £4 500 budgeted**

d **selling costs: £2 750 actual, £2 750 budgeted.**

2 **Explain the term 'management by exception.'**

3 **Define the term 'favourable variance'.**

1. a) £15 000 favourable; b) £2 500 adverse; c) £500 favourable; d) no variance. 2. Management by exception uses variances to assess and control managers' performance. 3. when actual costs are below, or actual revenue is above, the budgeted figure

57

Cost and profit centres

- Responsibility accounting is a fundamental part of budgetary control. It aims to ensure that each manager in the firm has a well-defined area of responsibility. As a result, all areas of the firm have someone responsible for their operation. This means that:
  - information about costs and revenues can be easily obtained
  - these costs and revenues can be closely monitored
  - decisions, based on this information, can be made about the performance of different areas of the business.
- A responsibility centre is a department or function under the control of a manager who is directly responsible for its performance. There are three types of responsibility centre:
  - a cost centre: something to which costs can be attributed
  - a profit centre: something to which costs and revenues can be attributed
  - an investment centre: a profit centre whose performance is measured by its return on capital employed (ROCE).

EXAMINER'S TOP TIP
The way that the firm's total profit is shared between its products can depend on how the overheads are shared between these cost centres.

Cost centres

- A cost centre – anything to which costs can be separately attributed – may be in the form of:
  - a department or other location – e.g. transport department, buying department, warehouse, sales office
  - an item of equipment – such as a photocopier, welding machine, pressing machine, telephone, desk, stationery cupboard
  - an item of expenditure – e.g. stationery, petrol, advertising
  - a person – e.g. a supervisor, a manager, a driver.
- The size of the cost centre varies. Some cost centres will contain other cost centres: for example, the Sales Department may act as a cost centre, containing cost centres such as sales-force mobile telephones, sales stationery, and sales force travel expenses.
- Costs will be charged to the cost centre using cost codes. Information about these cost centres is likely to be collected in terms of their actual and budgeted costs, and any variances. The person responsible for the cost centre is only responsible for those costs that are controllable.

Profit and investment centres

- A profit centre is anything to which costs and revenues can be separately attributed. (If the organisation is non-profit-making, it will have revenue centres rather than profit centres.) This allows the profitability of the centre to be measured. As with cost centres, the manager of the profit centre must have some control over the revenues and costs.
- Profit centres tend to be larger than cost centres: for example, a particular product may be treated as a profit centre.
- An investment centre is linked with both profit and investment. It may consist of a number of different profit centres, and is therefore likely to be larger than a profit centre.
- For example, a range of products, each one treated as a profit centre, may share certain resources such as machinery, equipment and delivery vehicles. This product range may be treated as an investment centre, and the overall return on investment for the range can be measured against the resources used to make and sell these products. The investment centre manager will have some involvement with – and control over – investment policy.

Cost centres and product costs

- In <u>absorption costing</u>, all costs are eventually allocated to individual products. <u>Direct</u> costs can be allocated easily and accurately to products, because they are directly linked to them: for example, the cost of raw materials going into the products. <u>Indirect</u> costs (overheads), such as the overall cost of rent, need to be <u>apportioned</u> (shared) to products using some logical basis.
- How these overheads are shared affects how the performance of the firm's individual products is judged. For example, using the figures from the box below:

<u>The profit before overheads are apportioned to the two products is:</u>
- Jed £125 000 (£250 000 – £125 000)
- Kel £100 000 (£150 000 – £50 000).

- The overheads of £150 000 now need to be apportioned between the Jed and the Kel.

<u>Apportioning overheads on the basis of floor area used (50% and 50%):</u>
- Jed 50% of £150 000 = £75 000; Kel 50% of £150 000 = £75 000
- Overall profit: Jed £50 000 (£125 000 – £75 000); Kel £25 000 (£100 000 – £75 000).

<u>Apportioning overheads on the basis of number sold (2/3 and 1/3):</u>
- Jed 2/3 of £150 000 = £100 000; Kel 1/3 of £150 000 = £50 000
- Overall profit: Jed £25 000 (£125 000 – £100 000); Kel £50 000 (£100 000 – £50 000).

<u>Apportioning overheads on the basis of employees (1/3 and 2/3)</u>
- Jed 1/3 of £150 000 = £50 000; Kel 2/3 of £150 000 = £100 000
- Overall profit: Jed £75 000 (£125 000 – £50 000); Kel £0 (£100 000 – £100 000).

- The way in which these overheads are split between the two products affects their profit calculations. The results show that, depending on how the indirect costs have been apportioned, profit for the Jed varies from £25 000 to £75 000, and that for the Kel from £0 to £50 000.
Note that, in all cases, the total profit made is always £75 000.

- The way in which a firm's indirect costs are apportioned between its products can therefore influence decisions about these products.

Hawk Ltd makes and sells two products: the Jed and the Kel.
Revenues and costs for these products are:

		£000
Sales income:	Jed	250
	Kel	150
Direct costs:	Jed	125
	Kel	50
Total overheads:		150

Other information:

	Jed	Kel
Factory floor space used by each product (%):	50	50
Number sold of each product:	500	250
Employees working on each product:	20	40

EXAMINER'S TOP TIP
When explaining about cost control, you should discuss whether a cost is likely to be controllable or non-controllable.

Quick test

1 Explain the term 'responsibility accounting'.
2 What is the difference between:
  a a profit centre and a cost centre?
  b an investment centre and a profit centre?
3 Give two examples of likely cost centres for a car manufacturer.
4 What is 'absorption costing'?
5 Name three ways of apportioning indirect costs between products.

1. a system whereby each area of a business has a manager who is responsible for its operation 2. a) a profit centre accounts for revenues as well as costs b) an investment centre includes capital employed 3. e.g. transport department, shop-floor assembly line, paint shop, sales office 4. a method whereby all costs are eventually linked to particular product lines 5. number of employees, floor space, number sold

59

Finance and accounting

1 Merchant Ltd is a firm producing blank CDs and DVDs for use in the IT and entertainment industries. Explain the difference between direct and indirect costs, using Merchant Ltd to illustrate your answer. [6]

....

....

....

2 Using the following information, calculate and comment on the average total costs for Gabriel Ltd. [6]

Output (units)	Fixed costs (£)	Variable costs (£)	Total costs (£)	Average total costs (£)
1 000	200 000	15 000		
2 000				
3 000				
4 000				

....

....

3 Preece & Sons Ltd makes and sells a range of different products in both home and overseas markets. The company's new managing director wants to use break-even analysis 'to help us set and analyse our prices'. Analyse how effective break-even analysis might be to this business. [6]

....

....

....

....

4 Mills Brothers Ltd makes clothing. One of its product lines is a sports T-shirt, which it sells to retailers at £5.00 per T-shirt. The company's expected output of T-shirts is 75 000. Relevant costs for this product are:

		Showing all your workings, calculate:	
total fixed overheads	£150 000		
material cost per T-shirt	£1.25	**a** the contribution made per T-shirt	[2]
labour cost per T-shirt	£0.50	**b** the break-even level of output and revenue	[2]
other variable costs per T-shirt	£0.25	**c** the margin of safety at the expected production level.	[2]

....

....

....

....

5 Outline how the actions of (i) its debtors, and (ii) its creditors, may lead to a business experiencing cash-flow problems. Explain the action a business may take to overcome the problems identified. [6]

....

....

....

....

6 Mason and Dixon run a successful and profitable partnership as builders. The partners have been offered a contract to build several new houses on a housing development. If they take up this offer, they will need to borrow money in order to:
- buy materials and pay staff
- buy an expensive digging machine to excavate the site.

a Suggest and justify, for both of the above, **one** appropriate source of finance. Use a different source for each. [3]

....

....

....

....

b The partners have the option of leasing the digger, rather than buying it. State **two** advantages and **two** disadvantages of leasing this machine rather than buying it. [3]

....

....

7 Staple Ltd is a manufacturing company that makes shoes and sandals that are sold in high street stores throughout the UK.

a List **three** likely budgets this company will create. [3]

....

b Explain any links between the three budgets listed in **a)** above. [3]

....

....

....

c Give **two** advantages that Staple Ltd is likely to gain from the budgeting process. Use the three budgets listed in **a)** to illustrate your answer. [6]

....

....

....

....

8 Here is the budgeted and actual performance of King Ltd. Calculate the profit and variance figures, and suggest **one** possible reason for each variance. [10]

	Budget (£)	Actual (£)	Variances (£)
Sales	675 000	750 000	
Materials	155 000	165 000	
Labour	200 000	190 000	
Overheads	70 000	75 000	
Profit			

....

....

....

Total: /58

Organisational structure

Hierarchies

- The management of a business carries out a number of functions. These include:
  - <u>planning</u> its future performance and strategy
  - <u>co-ordinating</u> its various functions such as production, finance and sales
  - <u>controlling</u> its activities through techniques such as budgetary control.
- These activities are carried out within a management and organisational <u>structure</u>. There is no single ideal structure for an organisation. Influences on how it is structured include those shown in this diagram.
- The traditional <u>organisation chart</u> outlines the formal structure of the organisation, defining individual roles within the organisation and showing the number of layers in the hierarchy.

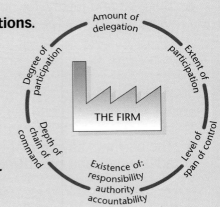

Functional and matrix management strategy

- Most organisations have been traditionally structured on the basis of the different business <u>functions</u> existing within the organisation. The main departments – for example, marketing, finance, production, human resources, and purchasing – often represent these functions.
- This approach is often referred to as '<u>line organisation</u>' since lines of responsibility are established clearly within the organisation. The organisational culture is known as '<u>role culture</u>' because individual roles for each staff member are clearly defined.

```
                        Board of directors
        ┌───────────────┬───────────────┬───────────────┐
   purchasing       production        finance        marketing
    manager          manager          manager         manager
   ┌──────┐       ┌──────┐          ┌──────┐        ┌──────┐
 buying  stores   shop            accounts        sales  marketing
 office  staff    floor staff     office staff    force  office staff
 staff
```

- Line structures are sometimes criticised for being bureaucratic, with the many layers in the hierarchy resulting in narrow spans of control.
- Many organisations have sought to remove layers in their hierarchy. This <u>de-layering</u> removes one or more of the layers, in an attempt to increase spans of control and improve communications.
- One approach has been to move away from functions and towards a team-based or project-based <u>matrix</u> approach. The matrix structure may combine the line structure with project or task-based <u>teams</u>, drawn from the various line departments in the organisation. It is often most effective in firms with wide spans of control and fewer hierarchical levels.
- Advantages claimed for the matrix approach include:
  - increased motivation, resulting from the team-based approach
  - the breaking down of traditional barriers that may exist between departments.

EXAMINER'S TOP TIP

Identify real-life examples of organisations having different structures.

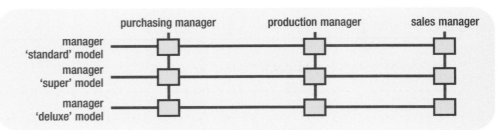

The Manager of each model will discuss sources of supply for their product's materials with Purchasing, liaise with Production concerning how their own model is made, and meet with the Sales manager to discuss how their particular model is being marketed.

Span of control and chain of command

The span of control is defined as the number of subordinates under the control of a manager. It is <u>narrow</u> when the manager has few staff to control, and <u>wide</u> when the manager has many staff. Influences on the size of the span include:
- the ability and degree of training of the manager and staff involved
- how <u>complex</u> the work is – the more complex the work, the narrower the span of control.

- Widening the span of control may benefit the firm through encouraging delegation, reducing supervision, improving communication and job enrichment. On the other hand, narrowing the span of control can help managers supervise employees more closely, and may result in less pressure on all staff.
- The vertical <u>chain of command</u> shown in the hierarchy indicates how control and <u>information</u> flow through it. As the organisation grows in size, the chain of command tends to become more complex since it runs through a number of levels in the hierarchy. Long chains of command are associated with <u>tall structures</u>. A firm with a tall structure is sometimes criticised because:
  - there can be a greater feeling of 'distance' between the top and bottom of the hierarchy
  - spans of control tend to be narrow
  - high-level decisions can take time to work through the organisation.
- As a result, many firms have sought to de-layer, producing <u>flat structures</u> with shorter chains of command.

Control flows DOWNWARDS — Board / Managers / Employees — Information flows UPWARDS

Centralise or decentralise?

- <u>Centralisation</u> encourages senior managers to make and communicate decisions quickly. However, a centralised structure discourages those lower in the hierarchy from making and taking decisions themselves. For example, the head offices of some national retailers decide pricing, layout and advertising policy on a national, rather than a local, basis.
- <u>Decentralised</u> structures, closely linked to delegation, are increasingly popular since they are often regarded as:
  - encouraging local, rather than national, decision-making
  - improving motivation through greater staff involvement
  - making <u>management by objectives</u> (MBO) more effective by setting personally devised objectives.

Authority, accountability and responsibility

- Managers need to <u>delegate</u> tasks to their subordinates, especially in larger organisations. If staff are to carry out these tasks successfully, they must be given the <u>authority</u> to carry out these tasks, and they have to take some <u>responsibility</u> for the tasks.
- Delegation that has been correctly given results in the employee becoming <u>accountable</u> to the manager for the delegated work done.

EXAMINER'S TOP TIP
Remember there is probably no one 'right' method for structuring and organising a business.

Quick test

1 *Define the terms 'span of control' and 'chain of command'.*
2 *What is 'de-layering'?*
3 *Give an example of delegation likely to occur in a large department store.*
4 *Use your answer to (3) to show the difference between authority and accountability.*

1. span of control: the number of staff under the direct control of an individual; chain of command: how information and control moves through the organisation. 2. the act of reducing the number of levels in a hierarchy 3. e.g. The store manager delegates responsibility for display to the departmental managers. The departmental manager delegates responsibility for promoting a certain product to departmental staff. 4. Departmental managers have the authority to display items, and are accountable to the store manager for this. The staff have the authority for the product's promotion (e.g. at point of sale), and are accountable to the departmental manager for this.

Motivation theory

Classical theory

- The Human Relations theorists who followed Taylor recognised that, when an employee is asked to carry out a task, and it is carried out badly, this may be due more to a lack of motivation rather than a lack of ability, training or incentive. They did not believe that pay was always the main motivator at work and concentrated more on the **needs** of staff rather than on the job being done, and on the work **environment**.

- These theorists concentrated on the nature of the work rather than the nature of the individual doing the work.

F W Taylor

- **F W Taylor** is regarded as the leading classical theorist. He used 'scientific management' principles to break jobs down into their separate elements. This led to the development of **work study** and **method study** principles, techniques closely linked with the **division of labour**, that were widely used in manufacturing industry in the last century, and are still found today in many firms involved in mass production.

- The work of Taylor and other classical theorists is now regarded as limited in scope, and was modified by the theorists that followed. Taylor's work ignored the negative effects associated with setting production and other targets linked to pay, and arguably encouraged the growth of the trade union movement, with the aim of protecting union members against what could be regarded as poor working practices.

- Taylor argued that **pay** was the main motivator, believing that it was the role of the manager to organise work in the most efficient way. As a result, his work led to bonus schemes and other pay **incentives** being devised to reward the most efficient workers.

Mayo

- **Elton Mayo** studied work groups operating at a company in Chicago. He regularly changed working conditions (e.g. the level of lighting) for one group being observed, and discovered that output still continued to rise even when the working conditions were made worse.
- Mayo discovered that a second group being observed also improved productivity, even though their working conditions were not being altered. His conclusion was that employees under observation appreciated the attention they were receiving, and – as a result – their self-esteem rose and their output increased. This is sometimes called the 'Hawthorne Effect', after the name of the company where the research took place.
- Conclusions from this and other work undertaken by Elton Mayo are that morale and output are influenced by factors such as:
  - effective communication
  - the existence of teamwork
  - the level of interest shown in their staff by managers.

EXAMINER'S TOP TIP Try to link the theories where possible: for example, study the links between Maslow's and Herzberg's work.

Maslow

- **Abraham Maslow** created his 'hierarchy of needs' in the 1940s. He argued that, at any given time, one group of these needs would be dominant in the workplace, and would need to be met before the member of staff concerned could proceed to the next (higher) group of needs.
- Maslow's findings suggest that work must give employees the opportunity to have these needs fulfilled, and therefore that employers should both recognise that their staff have a range of needs, and plan work that meets these needs.

Self-actualisation needs

Self-esteem needs

Social needs

Safety needs

Basic (or physiological) needs

Maslow's hierarchy of needs

Herzberg

- Frederick Herzberg created his **'Two-factor' Theory**, in which he analysed needs into two groups: **motivators** and **hygiene factors**. His motivators, based mainly on the content of work, relate closely to Maslow's higher order needs. Herzberg's hygiene factors are associated more with the working environment, and so link more closely to Maslow's lower order needs.

- Motivators help employees become more motivated, whereas by having their hygiene factors met, employees do not become demotivated.

Hygiene factors	Motivators
supervision	achievement
security	responsibility
working conditions	recognition
pay	promotion
status	the work itself

- Important conclusions from the work of Herzberg are that:
  - hygiene factors need to be present in work and are as important in their own way as are motivators
  - the importance of these hygiene factors is that they help employees avoid being demotivated at work – by themselves, they will not positively motivate employees
  - managers therefore need to provide hygiene factors, and also motivators in the form of satisfying work.

Vroom

EXAMINER'S TOP TIP

When writing about a theorist, remember to link the theory to the situation given in the question.

- Victor Vroom researched into the **strength** of a person's motivation. He devised a formula:

$$M = V \times E$$

M = degree of strength of Motivation
V = *Valence* (the importance of the reward to the person)
E = Expectation (how achievable the person expects the reward to be)

- Vroom's **Expectancy Theory** therefore suggests that the strength of someone's motivation depends on how **attractive** the reward is, and whether the person **expects** to achieve it.

Quick test

1 **Name the theories associated with the following people:**

 a **Abraham Maslow**

 b **Frederick Herzberg**

 c **Victor Vroom.**

2 **Give a work-based example for each level in Maslow's hierarchy.**

3 **Outline the key difference between FW Taylor and the later 'Human Relations' theorists.**

4 **Give two examples of:**

 a **motivators**

 b **hygiene factors.**

1. a) Hierarchy of needs b) Two-factor Theory c) Expectancy Theory 2. Food and drink (Basic); safe office (Safety); sports club (Social); promotion (Self-esteem); achieving full potential at work (Self-actualisation) 3. Taylor saw pay as always being the main motivator at work, which is disputed by later theorists. 4. a) e.g. responsibility, recognition b) e.g. supervision, security

Motivation in practice

- Organisations use a variety of methods in an attempt to overcome poor motivation levels amongst the workforce. Poor motivation leads to <u>alienation</u> amongst the staff, and is associated with poor timekeeping, increased absenteeism and more industrial disputes.

- As a result, organisations will try to avoid poor motivation occurring in the first place, for example through policies that focus on:

ensuring the firm's <u>leadership styles</u> are appropriate for its culture	reviewing the level of <u>pay</u> and other rewards being offered
providing opportunities for <u>teamworking</u> to take place	identifying the possibilities for <u>job enrichment</u> and related schemes.

- BT plc provides an illustration of the way staff can be involved in the work of a large organisation.

> 'We recognise that our people are critical to our success and believe that a reputation as a good employer helps win and retain an excellent workforce … We recently won the Parents at Work/DTI Employer of the Year Award for our approach to helping our people balance their work and home lives. We have a wide range of options to support individuals throughout their working life, including home working, alternative attendance patterns and career breaks. In addition, we recently introduced a flexible retirement policy …
>
> We encourage our employees to acquire shares in BT Group to enable them to share in our success …
>
> The BT New Ideas scheme, under which our employees are encouraged to put forward suggestions for improvements in the company's activities, generated more than 5,000 suggestions in the year, contributing to savings estimated to be around £30 million.
>
> We run CARE, an annual employee attitude survey, and encourage managers and their teams to put in place action plans to address the issues that it highlights …
>
> We are an equal opportunities employer and are committed to developing a working culture that enables all employees to make their own distinctive contribution …
>
> BT aspires to be a true learning organisation. We spend around £200 million a year on the training and development of our employees …'
>
> **Extracts from BT Annual Report**

EXAMINER'S TOP TIP
Make sure you know the differences between job enrichment, job rotation and job enlargement.

Job enrichment, rotation and enlargement

- <u>Job enrichment</u> is an increasingly popular way used to overcome poor motivation. It seeks to provide employees with work that is more interesting, and therefore more motivating, allowing employees to use their abilities fully.

- <u>Job rotation</u> may form one part of a job enrichment scheme. In job rotation, staff move between different jobs. A well-known example is in supermarkets, where some staff rotate between jobs such as checkout work, shelf stacking, and customer reception.

- A full job enrichment scheme involves staff working as a team – which provides the social element in the scheme – working on a range of different tasks. Herzberg suggested that a key feature of job enrichment involves working on a complete area of work, such as completing the full assembly of the inside of a car on a production line.

- Job rotation and job enrichment may result in <u>job enlargement</u>. This approach to work seeks to <u>increase the range of work done</u> by an individual.

Delegation and empowerment

- Under delegation, subordinates are given tasks to carry out. Empowerment extends the nature of delegation by giving the subordinates greater choice.
- With delegation, subordinates are given the authority to carry out certain tasks. If the subordinates are to be **empowered**, they will not only receive authority to carry out these tasks, but will also be given some involvement in deciding:
  - which **tasks** are to be carried out
  - when they are to be carried out
  - how they are to be carried out.
- Empowerment therefore provides the means by which staff can exercise some power over the work they do.

> **EXAMINER'S TOP TIP**
> Check company Annual Reports for examples of how they empower and involve their staff.

Involved & motivated colleagues

'One of the key drivers of our business is to be 'The Most Enjoyable Place to Work'. In March 2002 we were named 'Britain's Best Company to Work For' in a nationwide survey of UK businesses, big and small, by the Sunday Times, and again, this year, for the third year running, we featured in the Top 10 Best Companies to Work For List and scooped the prize for being the UK's best company for flexible working. The way we give our customers the legendary ASDA 'service with personality' is by it coming straight from the heart and this can only be achieved if people enjoy their work and feel they are respected and valued.

Listening is crucial to this and we have many ways of ensuring that all colleagues are listened to and their feedback acted upon, such as:

– the We're Listening Survey: the company's attitude survey where every month of the year at least 30 stores feed back their comments on their store, their management team, their pay and benefits, their training, motivation and teamwork. This ensures that there is constant feedback from the shop floor. We're Listening is also carried out in our head office and depots.'

Extract from ASDA website

Teamwork

The work of theorists such as Maslow and Mayo suggests that teamwork should be an important feature at work. It provides **flexibility** for both team members and managers, and helps **job enrichment** and similar schemes to become established.

- Factors that determine whether the team will be successful include:
  - how effective **communication** is in the team
  - the degree of **training** so all can do each other's work
  - how **cohesive** ('tight') the team is as a group
  - the **working atmosphere** within the team
  - the ability to **satisfy the needs** of all the team members.

Quick test

1 *Distinguish between job enrichment and job rotation.*

2 *State one benefit that effective teamwork should bring to:*

  a *the business*   b *the staff.*

3 *State the difference between delegation and empowerment.*

4 *Identify one effect that poorly motivated staff will have on the work of a business.*

1. job enrichment: teamwork providing team members with a range of tasks; job rotation: an individual moving between different jobs 2. a) helps establish job enrichment schemes b) provides increased flexibility 3. delegation: subordinate undertakes given tasks; empowerment: subordinate has some control over when and how to do the tasks 4. e.g. reduced output (quantity and/or quality)

Pay and financial incentives

The national minimum wage

- The UK now has a national minimum wage. The social purpose for introducing this was to provide employees with minimum standards and fairness in the workplace.
- Arguments in favour of a national minimum wage include:
  - encouraging businesses to compete on the quality of their products, and not on low prices based largely on low rates of pay
  - countering the concentration of low pay in certain sectors and groups – women, part-time workers, young people and some ethnic groups
  - reducing the pay gap between men and women at the bottom end of the earnings league.

- Rates are set by the independent Low Pay Commission, which first reported on the effects of introducing a national minimum wage in September 1999. It was introduced on 1 April 1999 at £3.60 per hour (£3.00 for 18- to 21-year olds). By October 2003 these rates had increased to £4.50 and £3.80 respectively, with plans to increase to £4.85 and £4.10 in October 2004.

Jobs paying less than £4.05 (22 and over) and £3.45 (18-21), Spring 2001

Male part-time 17%
Male full-time 13%
Female part-time 17%
Female part-time 53%

Source: Low Pay Commission

Wages and salaries

The traditional position of wage and salary earners is:

- There will be **pay differentials** in wages and salaries paid for different jobs in a firm. These differentials arise from differences in the:
  - level of qualifications required
  - amount of training needed
  - number of people who have the knowledge and skills to do the job
  - degree of danger or discomfort associated with the job.

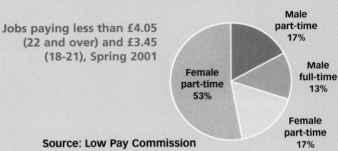

Wage	Type of pay	Salary
Manual	Typical work	Clerical
Weekly	Frequency of payment	Monthly
Payment for overtime	Nature of pay	Annual sum: no overtime

- Salaries and some wages are calculated on a **flat rate** or **time rate** basis. Salaries are annual, this yearly amount being divided into twelve equal monthly payments. Some wages are set at a fixed weekly rate. The advantage to the firm is that the individual's pay is **easy to calculate**, and can be accurately **budgeted** for.
- Wages may also be calculated on an **hourly** basis, with **overtime** being paid after the employee has worked a given number of hours. The higher overtime rate **encourages extra work** when output needs to be increased, although the total wage bill will be less easy to calculate.

EXAMINER'S TOP TIP
In questions about motivation, acknowledge that pay is an important motivator for many employees.

Incentive-based remuneration

Under a **piece-rate** scheme, employees are paid an **amount for each item made**.
The features of a piece-rate scheme are:
- employees are encouraged to work hard
- the harder-working employees receive more pay
- quality of the output may suffer through employees rushing their work
- high-quality control and supervision is therefore needed
- wastage levels may be high
- the total wage bill is difficult to budget for.

- **Performance-related pay** (PRP) is a scheme whereby staff regarded as being 'above average' receive higher pay. The pay and performance levels are established by setting targets for individual staff to achieve, and then comparing their performance against these targets.
Features of a PRP system include:
  - targets that should motivate staff
  - competition is encouraged
  - but this may be at the expense of teamwork and co-operation.

Annual Bonus Schemes

'All staff are now eligible to participate in the Annual Bonus Scheme. Bonus payments are based on measurable achievement of challenging financial and business targets, set in the corporate operating plan each year and approved by the Board.'

Extract from Marks & Spencer plc's Annual Report

Profit-sharing and share-ownership schemes

- Many large companies offer share-ownership schemes, which may be in the form of <u>Save as you earn</u> (SAYE) – staff buy shares through investing a set amount each month – or <u>share options</u> for senior staff, who can buy company shares at discount prices.

'Part of the ASDA Way of Working is to provide all colleagues with an opportunity to change and improve the business. We believe that this should extend to providing colleagues with a chance to share in the success of the company by receiving shares in it free of charge.

We have the largest Colleague Share Ownership plan (CSOP) of its kind in Britain. Around 92,000 colleagues now hold Wal-Mart share options through CSOP and Sharesave. The most recent payout (October 2002) saw almost 11,000 colleagues pocket £14.5 million worth of shares through both schemes.'

Extract from ASDA website

- <u>Profit-sharing</u> schemes reward staff with a share of the business's profit. These schemes therefore give employees the same financial interest as shareholders, which it is hoped will encourage hard work and loyalty.

Remuneration policy
'Profit sharing and SAYE schemes, encouraging employees at all levels to acquire and hold shares in the Company, are key elements of the policy. Employees have maintained their strong commitment to share ownership in recent years, and currently 42,700 employees hold approximately 31 million shares in their own right and 31,000 employees hold options on 78 million shares under the SAYE scheme.'

Extract from Marks & Spencer plc's Annual Report

Fringe benefits

- These 'perks' can influence the level of job satisfaction, and <u>encourage staff loyalty</u>. Examples include:
  - company cars and expense accounts
  - subsidised membership and travel schemes
  - low interest-rate loans
  - buying the firm's products at discounted prices.

EXAMINER'S TOP TIP
When discussing payment methods, recognise that they all have advantages and disadvantages.

Quick test

1 *Give one key difference between a flat-rate payment system and an incentive-based one.*
2 *List three examples of fringe benefits.*
3 *Explain one argument for introducing the national minimum wage in the UK.*
4 *Outline one advantage to a firm from introducing a profit-sharing scheme for its staff.*
5 *Give one advantage and one disadvantage to a business from operating a piece-rate payment scheme.*

1. flat-rate: fixed amount per week or month; incentive-based: variable amount, depending on meeting targets. 2. e.g. company cars, subsidised meals, discounted prices for the firm's products. 3. to reduce pay differentials between men and women at the lower end of the earnings scale. 4. gives staff the same financial incentive as shareholders, so loyalty is encouraged. 5. advantage: incentive to work hard; disadvantage: increased quality control and supervision costs

Management and leadership styles

The role of managers

- In the early twentieth century, <u>Henry Fayol</u> identified key management functions as:
  - <u>planning</u> – forecasting sales, labour requirements, etc.
  - <u>controlling</u> – by comparing actual against expected performance
  - <u>organising</u> – the key resources of the organisation
  - <u>commanding</u> – staff and resources
  - <u>co-ordinating</u> the above functions.
- These are still regarded as important activities for managers to undertake. More recent theorists have suggested other roles.
  - <u>Peter Drucker</u> has argued that <u>motivating</u> and <u>developing</u> staff, and setting up good <u>communication</u> systems, are important management skills.
  - <u>Charles Handy</u> suggests modern businesses, to stay competitive, need managers with the <u>Triple I</u> – **I**ntelligence, **I**nformation and **I**deas.

> **EXAMINER'S TOP TIP**
> Be prepared to acknowledge that one leadership style is not necessarily better than any other.

The main leadership styles

- Analysis of management and leadership styles is important because these influence how well people do their jobs.
- <u>Democratic</u> managers, often linked with McGregor's Theory Y (see below) and Herzberg's motivators, will guide and support subordinates, and will also actively involve the group in decision-making.
- <u>Autocratic</u> managers – who may share FW Taylor's view of staff being motivated primarily by pay and incentives – will not allow group involvement in the decision-making process, making decisions themselves.
- <u>Paternalistic</u> managers – who may be influenced by Maslow's lower order needs – may follow similar autocratic principles, although some group involvement in decision-making is likely, and a 'fatherly eye' is kept on group members, e.g. through providing additional facilities and showing an interest in individual careers.
- *Laissez-faire* managers allow group members to work as a group, preferring to stand back rather than become directly involved.
- There is not necessarily one 'best' leadership or management style. The choice of style is influenced by a number of factors.

- The effects of each of these styles are shown in the table.

The organisation's size and complexity

The extent and quality of staff training

The culture of the organisation

The extent and quality of management training

Personal preferences of the manager

The organisation's market

Leadership style

Autocratic	Democratic
• The manager is separated from the group.	• The manager is almost a group member.
• Communication tends to be one-way.	• Communication tends to be two-way.
• One person only makes decisions.	• Decisions are jointly made.
• Decisions can therefore be made quickly	• This may make decision-making slower
• – but there is no consultation.	• – but consultation has taken place.
• The group is not responsible for its actions	• The group is responsible for its actions
• – and is not encouraged to think for itself.	• – and is encouraged to think for itself.

Paternalistic	Laissez-faire
• The manager 'mothers' the group.	• The manager leaves the group alone.
• Communication is primarily one-way.	• Communication tends to be two-way.
• One person usually makes the decision.	• Decisions are left to the group.
• Decisions are therefore quick	• This may make decision-making slower
• – and the group may have been consulted.	• – and the manager's expertise is not used.
• The manager creates a sense of belonging	• The group is responsible for its actions
• – but the group may feel 'smothered'.	• – but may find it difficult to agree on policy.

McGregor

- <u>Douglas McGregor</u> explored two opposite extreme attitudes to do with work. His work focused on the attitudes of managers rather than employees.

Theory X	Theory Y
McGregor's Theory X manager assumes that staff dislike work and will therefore avoid it where possible.	McGregor's Theory Y manager assumes that staff enjoy work and wish to exercise their own initiative and control.
The manager assumes staff prefer to be directed rather than accept responsibility.	The manager assumes staff welcome responsibility, given they will be suitably rewarded.
This suggests that organisational objectives must be directed towards ensuring staff work, arguing for an <u>authoritarian</u> approach to management.	This suggests a more <u>democratic</u> form of management exists, with managers involving staff in decisions.
This view can be linked with the work of FW Taylor and other 'classical' theorists.	This view is more closely associated with the work of theorists such as Maslow and Herzberg.

- McGregor's analysis suggests that managers need to treat their staff as individuals, exploring what motivates them to work.
- In a dynamic (change) environment, the Theory X manager seeks to impose the change on staff, hoping to minimise resistance to this change.
- The Theory Y manager, on the other hand, will seek to involve staff in planning for change to take place, expecting them to be motivated by the changing work environment.

Likert

- <u>Rennis Likert</u> argued for a <u>participative</u> approach to management. He suggested there were four main leadership styles:

1 <u>exploitative authoritarian</u> – the use of 'the stick' to force employees to follow orders and instructions

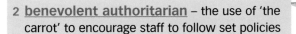

3 <u>consultative</u> – based on two-way communication, although decisions still tend to be made by top managers

2 <u>benevolent authoritarian</u> – the use of 'the carrot' to encourage staff to follow set policies

4 <u>participative</u> – staff are fully involved in setting targets and making decisions.

EXAMINER'S TOP TIP

Management styles should change as the business's situation and environment changes.

Quick test

1 List: a the five functions of management according to Fayol

    b one additional function identified by Drucker.

2 What are the three 'I's in 'Triple I'?

3 State one feature of:

    a democratic leadership   b laissez-faire leadership.

4 Name a theorist closely associated with:

    a Theory X and Theory Y   b participative management

    c 'Triple I'.

1. a) planning, controlling, organising, commanding and co-ordinating b) motivating staff, developing staff, setting up good communication systems 2. Ideas, Intelligence and Information 3. a) e.g. group involvement in decision-making b) e.g. the group can make decisions without involving the manager 4. a) McGregor b) Likert c) Handy

Workforce planning

- **Workforce planning is one area only of <u>human resource management</u> (HRM). The HRM function is found in all organisations, often as a specialist department. Key areas of HRM are:**

Area	Purpose
Workforce planning	To anticipate and plan staffing requirements
Recruitment and selection	To bring in new staff as and when required; to obtain the best people for the firm
Training and development	To review and develop staff skills; to encourage staff to achieve their potential
Appraisal	To review existing skills; to set goals for staff; to reward staff for achieving these goals
Welfare	To help staff satisfy their work-related personal needs
Consultation and negotiation	To communicate the firm's policies; to motivate staff through involvement; to identify and deal with staff concerns

Influences on the workforce plan

- The main function of workforce planning is to ensure the firm has the right **number** of staff of the right **quality**, in the right **place** and at the right **time**.
- Workforce planning should therefore ensure:
  - production and other functions can be carried out in the firm
  - productivity and other labour-related targets are met
  - budgeted labour costs are set, are realistic, and are controlled in practice.
- Overall, workforce planning should enable the firm to meet the workforce requirements identified in its corporate plan.

The workforce strategy of a firm is influenced by **<u>supply and demand</u>**.

If the supply of labour exceeds the firm's demand for it:	If the firm's demand for labour is greater than the labour supply:
• Redundancies may occur	• Recruitment costs will rise
• 'Natural wastage' will be allowed	• Retraining of some existing staff is required
• Early retirement schemes may be set up	• Labour is a principal budget factor
• Staff may be redeployed or retrained	• The firm may offer higher wages

- Workforce plans may be based on a **<u>STEP</u>** analysis of the influences on recruitment and retention of staff.
  - **<u>Social</u>** influences include: more women postponing the start of a family, and/or wishing to stay in employment; more people seeking part-time and flexible work.
  - **<u>Technological</u>** influences include: greater use of computers and information/communications technology at work.
  - **<u>Economic</u>** influences include: the UK replacing primary (e.g. agriculture) and secondary (manufacturing) jobs with tertiary (service) jobs.
  - **<u>Political</u>** influences include: government training schemes; free movement of labour in the EU; the effect of the Working Time and other Directives.

EXAMINER'S TOP TIP
Apply STEP analysis, in the context of workforce planning, to a firm you know.

Labour turnover (LTO)

- LTO calculations provide an important source of information for a firm. LTO will take place in any firm, and a certain level of LTO is of benefit to a firm because **new staff** are a source of **new ideas** and **new work** practices.
- Too high a level of LTO is a problem for the firm, since new staff need to be **recruited** (at a cost) and **trained** (at a cost). There is also a **lack of continuity** within the firm, and there can be a negative effect on the morale and motivation of those staff who remain.
- Some firms, on losing staff with certain skills, may find there is a **skill shortage**, which makes it difficult to recruit replacement staff who possess the same skills. In such cases the firm may offer financial and other **incentives** for existing staff to remain in post.

EXAMINER'S TOP TIP
Memorise the LTO formula, and remember that a certain level of LTO can actually be good for a firm.

- High LTO in a firm may be an indicator of one or more 'ills' in the firm, including:
  - low staff morale
  - uncompetitive pay rates in the locality
  - poor working conditions
  - limited promotion prospects.
- A business can calculate its LTO from the formula:

$$LTO = \frac{\text{Number of leavers in the period*}}{\text{Average number employed in the period}} \times 100$$

(* This figure is usually adjusted to take account of the number of **unavoidable** leavers, such as those dismissed or choosing to retire.)

- The HRM staff may create **retention profiles**, which group staff according to the year they joined, to give a more detailed profile of the workforce and how long staff members have been with the organisation.

Demographic and other trends

- Firms can use EU and UK government statistics to identify present trends and to forecast future trends in the labour force.
- One important labour trend has been the increase in participation rates for women over the past 25 years. Other changes, such as the greater numbers going into higher education, and the increasing popularity of early retirement, have led to fewer people being available for work, which has affected the overall labour market.
- Within the labour market, recent trends that affect the employment and workforce plans of organisations, include:
  - **more part-time and temporary work** – at present, two in every five workers are outside permanent employment
  - **increased flexible working** – flexitime, job sharing and other flexible work schemes have proved popular, especially with 'two-income' households.

Future trends can be estimated: for example, statistics from the Office for National Statistics suggest that:
- the UK population is expected to increase from 59.8 million in 2000 to nearly 65 million by 2025
- two-thirds of this expected increase will result from inward migration
- the UK's population remains an ageing one, with the mean age expected to rise from 38.8 in 2000 to 42.6 by 2025
- for the first time, from 2007 there are expected to be more pensioners than children.

- These changes suggest that the number of people of working age will rise by about 6 per cent, from 36.9 million in 2000 to 39 million in 2011. Firms can therefore use this information to predict how these changes will influence their future workforce needs.

Quick test

1 List five functions of the HRM Department in a large company.
2 How is labour turnover calculated?
3 What is the main purpose of workforce planning?
4 State two current trends in the UK labour market.
5 What is a retention profile?

1. workforce planning; recruitment and selection; training and development; staff welfare; consultation and negotiation   2. number of (unavoidable) leavers in a period as a percentage of number employed   3. to have the right staff with the right skills in the right place at the right time   4. increased numbers of women seeking work; increased number of part-time jobs   5. an analysis of staff showing how long they have been with the firm

Recruitment, selection and training

- The purpose of recruitment is to obtain suitable staff with appropriate skills. Recruitment needs will be identified in the organisation's workforce plan.
- A job description and a person specification are normally created when recruiting staff.

The job description contains:
- the job title
- the location and nature of the work
- an outline of the job tasks
- conditions of employment

The person specification contains:
- necessary experience
- qualifications that are needed
- any special skills required
- physical/other characteristics needed

- When recruiting staff, a decision has to be taken whether to use external sources, internal sources, or both. The decision is made on grounds of cost, and whether specialist recruitment firms are needed – for example, if senior staff need to be 'headhunted'.
- Internal recruitment occurs when someone already working in the business is recruited: perhaps a part-timer who now wants the job full time, promoting someone, or recruiting from another department (e.g. as a result of retraining)
- With external recruitment, an employee is recruited from outside the firm: through advertising in local or national papers, or specialist publications, or by contacting and using Job Centres or private employment agencies.

Internal	External
Internal recruitment is less expensive; it means the person is known to the firm and will be familiar with work practices; and staff morale may improve as a result.	External recruitment is more expensive, but it does not limit the firm's choice of employee, and brings new ideas into the firm from outside.

- Many businesses review the efficiency of their recruitment process by calculating the recruitment cost per appointment.

EXAMINER'S TOP TIP
Recruitment and selection are often grouped together: remember they are related but distinct HRM functions.

Selection

- To select candidates, the person specification is compared with details in the candidate's application form and/or the curriculum vitae (CV). Suitable candidates are then placed on a shortlist, their references are checked, and then – assuming the references support the candidate – asked to attend an interview.
- Interviewing remains the most frequently used method of selection. Interviews are a two-way event:

The interviewer can assess:	The interviewee can assess:
views, opinions and attributes	work conditions and resources
communication skills	prospects
physical appearance	the working atmosphere

- Although the interview has the advantage of being a two-way process, it is **not reliable** on its own as a selection method. It is subjective, relying on the interviewer's judgement, and there is not necessarily a link between the ability to do well in an interview and the ability to do the job well.
- Due to the weaknesses of the interview process, firms may use additional selection techniques. These may test a candidate's:
  - intelligence – tests that assess reasoning, or a specific area such as numeracy
  - aptitude – tests based on the ability to do tasks associated with the job
  - personality – psychometric testing of the candidate's personality, attitudes and beliefs.

Training and development

- Training attempts to improve the ability of employees to do their current jobs. Development seeks to help employees achieve their full potential. The firm's goals are to improve workforce skills, morale and motivation, which helps achieve its other objectives such as customer satisfaction. The government has encouraged UK business to invest in training – for example, by setting up the <u>Investors in People</u> (IiP) scheme.

> *'In February 2001, BT achieved re-registration as an Investor in People (IiP), against the new "outcomes based" IiP standards. We are one of the largest companies to measure up to this challenging test …*
>
> *All BT staff interviewed were very clear about their roles and the contribution they make to the company's objectives.'*
>
> **Extract from BT plc website**

- <u>Induction</u> training introduces a new member of staff to the firm and to the team, and the team to the new employee. Induction often includes: a tour of the firm, an outline of the firm's history and situation, meeting and discussions with relevant managers and staff, and identifying initial training and other needs.
- An effective induction training programme should motivate the new employee, and lead to productive work being done as soon as possible.
- <u>Internal</u> ('on-the-job') training is where employees learn as they work. This training is normally limited to the content and skills needed to carry out the employee's particular job.
  <u>External</u> ('off-the-job') training takes place when staff attend off-site training schemes, run at local colleges or other specialist training agencies.
- <u>Appraisal</u> is a formal assessment of staff performance and needs. The main objectives of an appraisal system are to:
  - establish links between the organisation's objectives and the contributions made by individual staff
  - provide feedback on present performance and achievement
  - improve performance and achievement in the future
  - give staff an opportunity to contribute to their own development
  - identify suitable staff for promotion and/or merit pay increases.
- The costs of <u>not</u> training include poor productivity and production levels, a lower quality product, increased absenteeism, and more accidents. This is likely to result in <u>demotivated staff</u> and <u>dissatisfied customers</u>.
- Appraisal is often linked with <u>management by objectives</u>, where achievement is measured against set targets and stated objectives.

Internal training:	**External** training:
• is easy to plan and organise	• removes job and work distractions
• meets the trainee's needs	• introduces new ideas
• can be inexpensive	• uses specialist trainers
• disrupts work for employee and trainer	• usually costs more
• uses non-specialist trainers	• tends to be theoretical not practical
• reinforces any poor work practices	• takes the employee away from work
• does not introduce new work methods	

STAFF APPRAISAL SCHEME

Name of appraisee: . . . .   Name of appraiser: . . . .

PRIORITY KEY PERFORMANCE AREAS

PERFORMANCE OBJECTIVES   TARGETS AGREED   METHOD OF MEASUREMENT

Agreed: . . . .   Agreed: . . . .
    Appraiser   Appraisee

Date: . . . .   Date: . . . .

EXAMINER'S TOP TIP
Link your recruitment, selection, training and development points to the wider objectives of the organisation.

Quick test

1 **Name three types of test that may be used at interview.**
2 **State two costs associated with not training staff.**
3 **Distinguish between recruitment and selection.**
4 **Explain the difference between a job description and a person specification.**

1. personality; aptitude; intelligence   2. lower productivity, lower quality product, increased absenteeism, more accidents   3. recruitment: attracting suitable staff; selection: choosing suitable staff for jobs   4. Job description: details of the job; person specification: qualities needed to do the job

75

People in organisations

1   TootyFrooty Ltd makes fruit drinks at several factories in the UK. It has recently introduced a new banana-flavoured soft drink that is not selling well. The Production Manager has complained that he spends most of his time having to co-ordinate production across the different factories, and that his span of control is too narrow. The present organisation chart for TootyFrooty Ltd is shown below.

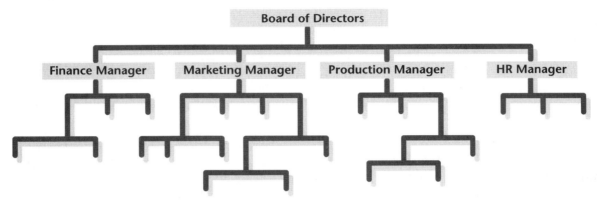

   a   Explain possible problems for TootyFrooty Ltd resulting from narrow spans of control.   [3]

   ....

   ....

   b   Suggest an alternative organisational structure that this company might consider.   [3]

   ....

   ....

2   Extra Ltd makes parts for cars and other vehicles. These parts are mass-produced on assembly lines in an old, badly designed and poorly ventilated part of the site. Staff working on these lines have a higher than average absenteeism record, and a recent attempt to improve productivity by offering financial incentives has not worked.

   a   Suggest, referring to appropriate theories, why the assembly-line staff might suffer from poor motivation.   [4]

   ....

   ....

   ....

   b   Outline ways in which the motivation of these staff might be improved.   [4]

   ....

   ....

   ....

3   a   Identify **two** features of autocratic management.   [2]

   ....

   b   Outline **one** business situation in which an autocratic style might be appropriate.   [2]

   ....

Irene Morrison was pleased when her business exceeded its profit target, especially when the firm had just launched a new product (for which Irene is solely responsible), and the firm had been experiencing extremely high labour turnover. Irene discusses matters with her staff, although she then takes all decisions herself. Irene has recently appointed Adil Mahmood to the post of Human Resources Manager, and Adil plans to introduce teamwork into the business.

c) Outline how a teamwork approach may help Irene in her present situation. [3]

....

....

d) Assess whether a more democratic leadership style might be appropriate in Irene's situation. [4]

4 Clinton McCall owns and runs a telephone call centre, employing staff to supply car-insurance quotations to people calling the centre. Virtually all staff in the centre sit in front of a computer screen all day. Each person will receive a call, enter the potential customer's information into a computer, and then give an insurance quote in the hope the customer will buy this insurance. Staff were initially paid a fixed weekly wage for their work.

After several months, Clinton noticed a fall in the number of insurance policies sold. He therefore introduced a new payment system: staff are now paid a small fixed weekly wage, and receive commission on each insurance policy they sell to callers. Business improved dramatically in the first months of the new payment scheme, but recently staff absenteeism has become a major problem.

Using the information given above:

a) Give **one** reason why the first payment method used may have led to a fall in the number of insurance policies being sold. [2]

....

b) Explain why Clinton's business initially benefited from the introduction of the new payment scheme. [3]

....

....

c) Suggest **one** reason why staff absenteeism has increased in recent months. [3]

....

....

d) What scope does Clinton have to introduce job rotation or job enrichment in order to reduce staff absenteeism? [4]

....

....

5 A large insurance company is finding that its existing employees do not have the appropriate skills for the future. Examine how it may overcome this problem. [6]

....

....

....

6 Explain, using examples, why job descriptions and person specifications are likely to be important to a large national food retailer. [6]

....

....

....

Total: /49

Size and scale

The size of an organisation can be measured using a range of indicators. These include:

- profits
- turnover
- capital employed
- number of employees.

- Most firms seek to grow in size. Large size brings with it not only economies of scale, but also improved survival prospects, better capacity utilisation of resources, and an increased sense of power and status.

An organisation can achieve growth in two ways:

1 External growth (*integration*)

Two firms join together, by

Merger, when the firms agree to combine their assets   **OR**   **Takeover**, when one firm obtains a controlling interest in another

2 Internal growth (*organic growth*)

The firm expands using its own resources by:

retaining its profits

which preserves its liquid assets (cash)

which are then invested in additional fixed assets

which improve its production capacity

and increase its market share

- **Takeovers and mergers are ways to increase in size quickly. This integration may be:**

Horizontal	Vertical	Lateral (conglomerate)
Firms in the same industry and the same stage of production.	Firms in the same industry at different stages of production.	Firms from different industries join together.
Large-scale production (economies of scale) and greater market share.	Protects controls outlets and supplies.	Diversification of products and markets spreads risk.

EXAMINER'S TOP TIP

Identify and memorise some real-life examples of horizontal, vertical and lateral integration.

Internal economies of scale

- These occur when the increase in a firm's size and the scale of its operations reduces its unit costs. Although total costs – production, marketing, or administration – increase, the average cost per unit falls because the costs are being spread over a greater output.
- Internal economies of scale can be evaluated financially because they can be quantified (measured). There are different economies of scale, largely based on the various functions of a typical business.
  - Economies of **increased dimensions** – these arise from an increase in size: for example, a double-decker bus contains twice the passengers but still only needs one driver.
  - **Financial** economies – larger firms are thought to be more financially stable, therefore find it easier to borrow money, often at cheaper rates.

- **Managerial** economies – larger firms can employ more specialist (and efficient) managers.
- **Marketing** economies – larger firms can employ specialist advertising agencies, and can spread marketing costs over much greater output.
- **Purchasing** economies – bulk-buying discounts can be obtained as a result of larger orders, reducing the unit cost of materials, and also more favourable credit terms can be agreed with suppliers.
- **Risk-bearing** economies – a wider product range allows the firm to spread risk more successfully.
- **Technical** economies – larger firms can afford to invest more in research and development, and can also afford more specialist and efficient technology.

External economies of scale

- These result from an increase in size of the industry, rather than the firm. External economies most commonly occur when the industry is located in a limited area geographically: examples include car-making (traditionally the West Midlands), and pottery and ceramics (Stoke-on-Trent).
- All firms in the industry may benefit from these economies, examples of which are:
  - <u>training</u> – local training providers concentrate on the skills and knowledge required in the particular industry
  - <u>support</u> – local firms provide specialist support, e.g. producing components needed in the industry
  - <u>information</u> – local chambers of commerce and trade associations focus on the industry's needs.

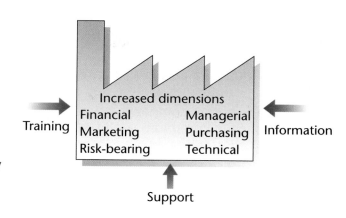

Internal and external economies of scale

Diseconomies of scale

EXAMINER'S TOP TIP

Remember that, with economies of scale, unit costs fall but total costs may still rise.

- There are limits to the amount of growth for any business: the most common limitation is the level of demand for its products.
- After the business achieves a certain size, it may find that its unit costs start to increase: it is now starting to experience diseconomies of scale.
- There may be a number of reasons for these diseconomies:
  less efficient and slower communication, due to the increased number of levels in the firm's hierarchy
  a longer chain of command, which means greater bureaucracy ('red tape') and slower decision-making.
- The overall effect of diseconomies of scale is to make the firm become less competitive through lower efficiency, poor staff morale, a weaker management function, and slower reaction to changing market conditions.

Survival of the small firm

Small firms survive despite not benefiting from economies of scale. Reasons for their survival include:
- offering a specialised product and operating in a niche market
- having a local demand.

Quick test

1 State the main difference between internal and external economies of scale.
2 List three internal economies of scale.
3 Give one illustration of a financial economy of scale.
4 Identify one diseconomy of scale.
5 Name the type of integration illustrated by the following examples:
   a two car manufacturers merge
   b a tobacco company takes control of a food-processing business
   c a brewery takes over a chain of public houses.

1. internal: found within a firm; external: exist in the industry   2. e.g. purchasing, risk-bearing, marketing   3. e.g. being able to obtain loans at a lower rate of interest   4. e.g. slower communication through the firm's hierarchy   5. a) horizontal   b) lateral   c) vertical

Capacity utilisation

High capacity

- A firm's productive capacity is based on the <u>resources</u> it has. Premises, machinery and equipment, and labour are the key productive resources.
- Capacity utilisation compares how these resources are being used to produce the <u>actual output</u>, which is compared with the expected <u>maximum output</u> for these resources. When all resources are working at <u>full capacity</u> there is 100% capacity utilisation.
- The formula for calculating the capacity utilisation % is:

$$\frac{\text{Actual output}}{\text{Maximum output capacity}} \times 100$$

- The capacity utilisation of a firm that can make 500 000 products a month, but which only makes 400 000 products a month, is therefore 80%. This means that 20% of its resources are being non-productive. This is one reason why it is important to calculate a firm's capacity utilisation.
- The higher the capacity utilisation, the lower the firm's unit costs will be. There are two reasons for this:

its <u>fixed costs are spread over higher output</u> (resulting from the higher capacity utilisation)	higher capacity utilisation should encourage <u>economies of scale</u> such as bulk-buying, which will reduce unit variable costs.

- For example, an unsuccessful football club with a 20 000-capacity stadium rented for £10 000 a year from the local council, may only currently attract 5 000 supporters: a 25% capacity utilisation. If next season the club is successful, and attracts capacity gates (100% utilisation), it still only has to pay the same £10 000 rent. Furthermore, it can buy food for sale at the match at lower prices (bulk-buying), and pay less for the print-run of its programmes (the set-up printing costs are spread over far more programmes).

> **EXAMINER'S TOP TIP**
> Increasing capacity utilisation should reduce unit costs; lower utilisation is likely to increase unit costs.

Low capacity

- Low-capacity utilisation suggests <u>low efficiency</u> and <u>idle resources</u>. As a result, higher unit costs have to be absorbed, or the firm may have to increase its prices, leading to <u>reduced competitiveness.</u>
- The firm may be able to increase capacity utilisation by:
  - increasing the demand for, and awareness of, its products (e.g. through more advertising)
  - cutting excess capacity by 'right-sizing' measures of rationalisation – e.g. 'natural wastage' of staff, or selling surplus machinery and equipment.
- The decision on whether to cut excess capacity is influenced by the causes of the excess capacity. If the cause is temporary – for example, low demand for a seasonal business – the managers may decide to accept surplus capacity for the period.

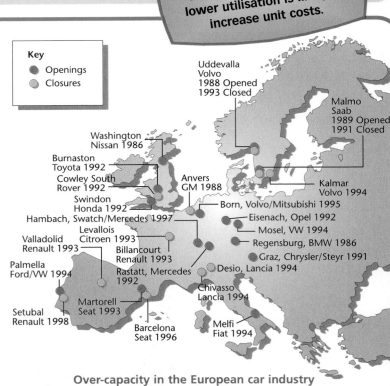

Over-capacity in the European car industry

Problems of full capacity

- A firm working at full capacity is likely to have its fixed costs at their lowest, and is using its productive resources fully.
- Working at or near full capacity will create certain pressures.
  - There is pressure on its **human resources** – e.g. staff may suffer from stress or fatigue, leading to increased absenteeism and low morale.
  - There is pressure on **other resources** – e.g. maintenance is difficult to carry out as a result of high machine usage, which may lead to machine breakdown through over-use.
  - It is difficult or impossible to take on extra work, which can lead to a loss of customer goodwill.
- Most firms therefore choose not to work at 100% capacity, allowing some 'slack' for periods of greater demand so they can meet additional customer requirements and preserve customer goodwill. They are also able to service machines and equipment, and staff are likely to have higher morale as a result of fewer work pressures.
- A firm working at full capacity can increase capacity through employing more resources.
  Examples where this is regularly done include seasonal businesses, where employees may be taken on for a fixed term (e.g. the 'summer season' in holiday towns and centres), or where equipment is hired for the duration of the busy season (e.g. agricultural fruit-picking machinery).

EXAMINER'S TOP TIP
Remember that there are disadvantages, as well as advantages, of operating at full capacity.

Changing capacity

- Falling demand for its products is likely to result in a firm having **excess capacity**. If this fall in demand is not simply seasonal, the firm will need to reduce its maximum capacity. To do so, it will examine its existing resources.
- The size and make-up of its **labour force** is a key factor. The firm has a number of options, including:
  - cutting certain shifts or stopping overtime
  - allowing for natural wastage to take place (employees leave and are not replaced)
  - asking for voluntary redundancies – though the firm will not wish to lose staff whose skills are valued and are in short supply
  - making certain staff compulsorily redundant.
- The firm may also rationalise its **fixed assets**.
  - Buildings may be sold off, or some space rented to other businesses.
  - Surplus machinery and equipment may also be sold off – many firms in fast-changing industries often hire these rather than buy them, which gives greater flexibility when demand levels change.

Quick test

1 Give one reason why a company seeks to increase its capacity utilisation.

2 How is capacity utilisation calculated?

3 Name three important productive resources.

4 A company with a capacity to make 5 500 units a week is presently making 3 575 units each week. Calculate its capacity utilisation.

5 Give two disadvantages associated with low-capacity utilisation.

6 Give one example of an industry where capacity utilisation varies seasonally.

1. e.g. to use resources more efficiently   2. actual output as a percentage of maximum output capacity   3. e.g. staff; premises; machinery   4. 3575 divided by 5 500 gives 65%.   5. e.g. resources used inefficiently; reduced competitiveness   6. hotels, entertainment industry, sports industry, agriculture, tourism

Production and productivity

Types of production

- **Production of products – goods <u>and</u> services – can be either <u>intermittent</u> or <u>continuous</u>.**
- **The three types of production are job, batch and flow (mass): a firm selects one to use largely on the <u>scale of production</u> required.**

EXAMINER'S TOP TIP

Think of products that are made using the three different production methods.

Job production

- This takes place when a single product is made to the customer's specification.
  Examples include 'one-off' construction projects such as the Severn and the Humber bridges.
  A firm involved in job production has to carefully consider the 'three **C**'s of:

Costs

Cash flow

Completion date

March
1 2 3 4
5 6 7 8

- The main characteristics of job production are:

> **a high-priced product**
> *made with*
> **equipment flexible enough to meet a number of needs and designs**
> *used by*
> **a highly skilled workforce**
> *controlled by*
> **centralised management**
> *who use a range of*
> **planning and control techniques**

- Although difficult to manage and co-ordinate, because of its 'one-off' nature, staff using job production are often highly motivated due to the variety of tasks, for which they can often use their full range of skills.
- Items made using job production are often expensive, as a result of employing highly skilled staff, buying expensive raw materials, and having to meet a range of one-off (e.g. planning) costs.

Batch production

- In batch production, a set number – a batch – of the product is made, and then production switches to making a different product.
- A batch may go through one part of the production process, before being moved onto the next: for example, all items in a batch of components may be assembled before the batch moves to the painting area.
- Examples of batch production include the manufacture of furniture, and certain foodstuffs such as bread and cakes.
- Batch and job production share similar characteristics, although batch production methods can benefit to a greater extent from economies of scale since costs can be spread over the number of items made in the batch.

| The batch of potatoes is *peeled* | → | The batch of potatoes is *cut into chips* | → | The batch is *cooked* |

Flow (mass) production

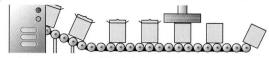

- Products that are <u>identical</u> and <u>standardised</u> are made in a continuous (mass production) process. Flow production is based on the principles of <u>specialisation</u> and the <u>division of labour</u>.
- In order for it to work, flow production relies on a <u>mass market</u> for its products. As a result, it is most closely associated with cars, consumer durables, and the mass-produced foodstuffs and home-improvement items found in the major high street and out-of-town stores.

products with lower profit margins than those made using job production

high numbers of semi-skilled labour

large capital investment in expensive and specialist machinery and equipment

The main characteristics of flow production are

a cost-effective approach to production, with costs controlled by standard costing and budgetary control methods

production layouts that allow the product to 'flow' from one section to the next

high productivity levels

As a result of the above, economies of scale occur.
- The gain in productivity from flow production has to be balanced by many drawbacks associated with it. These include:
  - a <u>lack of flexibility</u> of equipment and of labour – the effect is that the equipment and the workforce may become unemployed if the demand for the mass-produced item falls
  - <u>low morale</u> arising from staff having to do repetitive tasks all day, with little or no opportunity to use their initiative
  - the likelihood of a <u>major production stoppage</u> if any part of the flow-line fails, e.g. through equipment breakdown, or as the result of a labour dispute.
- These drawbacks have resulted in the development of the <u>lean production</u> methods that are now widely used in the production process.

> **EXAMINER'S TOP TIP**
> The drawbacks of using flow production largely come from its negative effects on employees.

Productivity

- The role of production is to turn inputs into output. Productivity assesses <u>how efficiently these inputs are being used</u>. Capacity utilisation is one indicator of productivity.
- <u>Labour</u> productivity is often measured. It can be calculated as:

$$\frac{\text{Output in the period}}{\text{Number of (full-time) employees}}$$

- Improved labour productivity leads to greater efficiency and, as a result, increased profitability.
- Labour productivity is greatly influenced by factors such as the level of <u>motivation</u> and the amount and quality of <u>training</u>.

Quick test

1. The 'three Cs' that need considering in job production are …
2. Give three drawbacks associated with mass production.
3. How is labour productivity calculated?
4. Classify these products according to their likely method of production:
   a. bread baked and sold by a local baker
   b. a new road bypassing a village
   c. jam made for, and sold by, a large-scale retailer such as Sainsbury's.

1. costs, cash flow and completion date 2. e.g. poorly motivated staff, inflexible equipment, the risk of complete shutdown if one area of the production line cannot continue 3. output in a period is divided by the number of employees 4. a) job b) batch c) flow (mass)

Stock control

The purchasing function

- Both manufacturing and non-manufacturing businesses have to make a variety of purchases.
- The main role of the purchasing function is that of <u>materials management</u>.

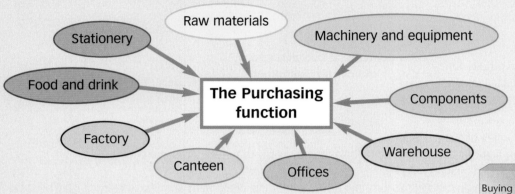

- The items to be obtained by Purchasing need to be bought at:
  - the correct <u>price</u>
  - the correct <u>quality</u>
  - the correct <u>quantity</u>.

Buying stock in bulk to achieve discount and ensure supply

Avoiding the cost of holding large quantities of stock

The purchasing balancing act

Stock and stock levels

EXAMINER'S TOP TIP
Link this topic to 'Lean production' and Just-in-time stock control.

- Why does a business need to hold stock, given that there are costs in doing so?

Stock category	Reason for holding	Costs of zero stock
Raw materials and work in progress	Production requirements must be met	Idle time for staff; machine down-time; production is delayed
Finished goods	Customer orders must be met	Loss of orders; lost customer goodwill; financial penalties
Consumables, e.g. stationery, spare parts	Production and sales functions need support	Production is stopped; sales cannot be made

- Efficient stock control is therefore based on identifying and holding the optimum stock. The firm will need to manage its stock efficiently, by using the oldest stock first – stock <u>rotation</u> – to minimise stock wastage.

Stock control using ICT

- More and more firms are using <u>information and communication technology</u> (ICT) to help manage and control their stock.
- An example is the <u>electronic point of sale</u> (EPOS) system that updates stock records instantaneously when a customer buys an item, and automatically places an order for replacement stock when it reaches a certain level.

Costs of having the wrong stock levels

- If the stock levels are too <u>high</u>, the firm will pay unnecessary holding costs, such as:
  - storage and store operation costs
  - insurance costs
  - interest charges on capital tied up in stocks
  - any costs arising from deterioration, obsolescence or theft.

- If the stock levels are too <u>low</u>, the firm cannot produce or sell its goods. There is an <u>opportunity cost</u> of being without stock, because the customer's order cannot be met, and the customer may be lost to a competitor.
- In the short term the firm may have to face financial penalties from customers by not being able to meet sales deadlines. Loss of customer goodwill is likely to reduce its profits and affect its survival in the longer term.

The <u>higher</u> the stocks, the less chance of running out

BUT

the firm faces higher stockholding costs

$\uparrow$

STOCK LEVELS

$\downarrow$

The <u>lower</u> the stocks, the lower the holding costs

BUT

there are increased risks of a 'stock-out'

EXAMINER'S TOP TIP
Remember that 'stock' is more than raw materials: it includes finished goods, work in progress, and stationery and other consumables.

Stock calculations

- <u>Economic order quantity</u> (EOQ) calculations will establish the most economical amount to buy. The calculation is:

$$EOQ = \sqrt{\frac{2od}{h}}$$

where
o = ordering cost of item,
d = (annual) demand for item, and
h = holding cost of 1 unit per annum

- If, therefore, the annual demand for an item is 10 000 units, it costs £15 per order, and the annual holding cost is £6 per unit, the EOQ is:

$$\sqrt{\frac{2 \times 15 \times 10\ 000}{6}} = 223 \text{ units}$$

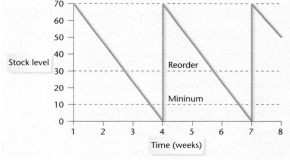

Stock control chart

- A <u>reorder level</u> is set, and is the level at which a new order must be placed.
- <u>Minimum stock</u> – also known as <u>buffer</u> stock – is the 'insurance' level of stock kept in case there are delays in receiving new stock.
- A <u>maximum stock</u> level is also set to indicate the figure above which stock should not go.

Quick test

1 State two costs of holding:

  a too little stock

  b too much stock.

2 What is the role of the Purchasing function?

3 In EOQ calculations, what do 'o', 'd' and 'h' refer to?

4 What is the link between stock rotation and stock wastage?

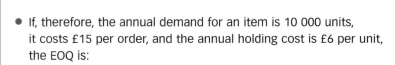

therefore should help keep stock wastage to a minimum.
unit holding cost. 4. Stock rotation ensures the oldest stock is used first. This reduces the chance of deterioration and obsolescence, and
correct price and time, the correct quality and quantity, and arranging delivery to the correct place. 3. Ordering cost, annual demand, and
1. a) e.g. loss of customer orders, lost production. b) e.g. higher storage and insurance costs. 2. materials management, buying at the

Lean production

- The 'lean-production' approach seeks to improve how a firm uses its resources in order to respond better to its market. Consumers want good-quality products, available when demanded, and offered at a competitive price. It is the role of lean production to meet these demands.

- Lean production is not solely concerned with the manufacturing process. It also considers the wider role of employees, and the benefits from making a quality product that is efficiently designed and marketed.

- The three main elements in a lean-production approach are the just-in-time (JIT) manufacturing and materials- management system, the total quality management (TQM) approach, and time-based management. It is also associated with <u>cell production</u> and <u>quality circles</u>.

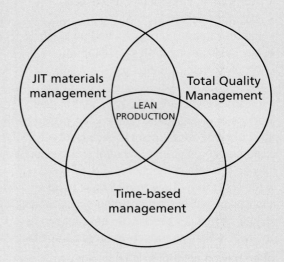

- An efficient lean production approach should:
  - <u>improve quality</u> – leading to greater customer satisfaction and higher profits
  - <u>increase productivity</u> – which has the effect of reducing labour costs per unit made or sold
  - <u>increase capacity utilisation</u> – so the firm's resources are being used to a fuller extent
  - <u>reduce wastage</u> – which cuts costs, and leads to more economical ordering
  - <u>cut stockholding costs</u> – reducing costs such as rent and the wages of store staff
  - <u>improve staff morale</u> – through an efficient system and an involved workforce.

Cell production

- This approach to manufacturing divides a continuous production line into distinct 'cells', each cell having a self-contained team of staff who make an identifiable part of the finished product. Each team is therefore responsible for part of the production process: this responsibility extends to areas such as health and safety within the cell.
- In cell production, the staff become **more involved** in the production process, and are therefore more motivated.

Time-based management

- Time-based management recognises that '**time is money**'. It attempts to find ways to save time, which will therefore reduce costs. A firm's managers are therefore encouraged to manage time in the same way that they manage other resources.
- Time-based management often concentrates on reducing the time it takes to make a product, to cut costs and make the product available to the consumer as quickly as possible. As a result:
  - production lead times are shortened
  - productivity improves
  - lower stock levels are needed
  - stockholding and production costs are reduced.

EXAMINER'S TOP TIP
The key features of lean production are an attempt to minimise costs and, at the same time, maximise quality.

Just-in-time (JIT)

- The traditional, 'just-in-case', approach is based on having buffer (minimum) stock levels in case something goes wrong. The JIT approach to materials purchasing and stockholding is based on the desire to reduce stockholding costs as far as possible by operating with a zero buffer stock. Using JIT, materials are delivered to the production line (or, for a retailer, to the store) just as they are needed – 'just in time'. In this way, stocks are minimised. JIT also has an <u>opportunity cost</u> benefit, of releasing space and resources for other use in the firm.

- The <u>kanban</u> system is associated with JIT. This system creates order cards for all stock items, one order card being released when a bin holding a stock item is empty. The item is then ordered from the supplier (or made internally). The kanban system helps the production area to avoid being full of stock items waiting to be used, thereby saving space.

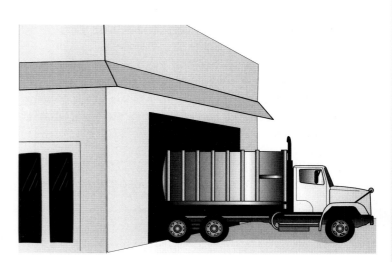

- <u>Manufacturers</u> who use JIT sometimes encourage suppliers to set up near the factory, to overcome the problems of delivering from a distance. <u>Retailers</u> operating a JIT system often rely on point-of-sale technology to update stock records and generate automatically orders for delivery.

- For a JIT system to operate successfully, a firm therefore needs suppliers who can deliver materials on time to meet the firm's production demands. Other factors influencing the success of a JIT scheme are:
  - the quality of the parts being delivered
  - the reliability of the delivery vehicles and state of the transport network
  - the influence of random factors such as bad weather or industrial action
  - the ability of the workforce to respond to any stock and manufacturing problems arising from the operation of the JIT system.

> **EXAMINER'S TOP TIP**
> Remember that, as well as ensuring stock arrives on time, there are other issues that affect whether just-in-time operates successfully.

Advantages of JIT	Disadvantages of JIT
● Lower stockholding costs	● Increased order costs
● Less wastage	● Total reliance on the supplier
● Improved cash flow and liquidity	● One failed delivery halts production
● Storage space is freed up	● The firm's reputation is in the hands of its suppliers

Quick test

1 Suggest two advantages associated with lean production.
2 What is the difference between 'just-in-time' and 'just-in-case'?
3 List the main elements of a lean-production approach.
4 Explain briefly the nature of cell production.
5 Give two advantages and two disadvantages associated with JIT.

1. e.g. improved product quality; increased labour productivity. 2. Just-in-time tries to operate with a zero buffer stock, whereas just-in-case allows for a buffer stock to be held. 3. JIT, TQM, time-based management, cell production, quality circles. 4. The production line is divided into self-contained 'cells'— teams making a definable part of the overall product. 5. advantages: e.g. lower stockholding costs, storage space is available for other use; disadvantages: e.g. order costs rise, and the firm is in the hands of its suppliers

Quality matters

- Firms need <u>customers</u> in order to survive and (if relevant) make profits. Customers need to be satisfied: if they are not, the firm will lose customer goodwill, and the customers will go elsewhere for their products.
- Good quality may bring a <u>competitive advantage</u> – an advantage it has over its competitors – to a firm. There are many firms known for their 'quality products', who rely heavily on this reputation.

- The effects of poor quality are often published in the mass media: reports in newspapers and TV consumer programmes such as 'Watchdog' that criticise a business will affect its survival chances.

Kaizen (continuous improvement)

– The company suggestion scheme ... is the most successful suggestion scheme in the UK. Founded in 1993 the scheme has received over 51,000 (around 5,200 a year, 100 a week) suggestions, comments and letters from colleagues.

– Colleague Circles meet every month in every store and feed into a quarterly divisional Colleague Circle and an annual national Colleague Circle where a colleague representative from every store puts the Board on the hot spot.

Extract from ASDA plc website

- The Kaizen philosophy argues that employees have two roles: carrying out their jobs, and looking for ways their jobs can be improved. This philosophy is not limited to production: all staff in all business functions can seek to improve the efficiency of what they do. Kaizen is therefore an investment in staff views and ideas, leading to a series of small changes that, in turn, lead to gradual improvements in working methods.
- For Kaizen to be implemented successfully, employees must be willing to contribute, and be prepared to work in teams. The firm's organisational culture must also be capable of supporting Kaizen, for example by allowing performance targets to be set, with performance being monitored against these targets.
- There are two recognised limitations to the Kaizen philosophy of continuous improvement.
  - Sometimes, major changes are necessary to overcome crises at the workplace: Kaizen's approach of continuous improvement will not lead to major changes being implemented quickly.
  - The law of diminishing returns can apply: there may only be a certain number of improvements that can be made to any work system, and the work systems in the greatest need of improvement will have been tackled first of all, leaving less important issues to be dealt with.

Quality control

- Quality control is an important feature of traditional production control. It focuses on identifying and scrapping poor-quality production. Its purpose is therefore to <u>maintain standards</u> by concentrating on:
  - preventing problems occurring in the first place
  - discovering poor-quality items before they are despatched
  - improving quality and quality-related procedures.

- There are two groups of costs associated with a quality-control system. Those directly related are the costs of inspection and testing, and training of staff. The costs indirectly linked are the costs of scrapped production, wasted labour time, having to make good poor workmanship, and loss of customer goodwill if poor quality products are not identified.

Quality assurance and quality circles

- Quality assurance seeks to ensure that customer satisfaction is achieved through quality standards being agreed, set and implemented throughout the whole organisation.
- Quality circles consist of groups of staff who have a common interest (e.g. being from the same work section), and who meet on a regular basis to discuss work-related matters. Quality circles are closely linked to the Kaizen philosophy.

Total quality management (TQM)

- Businesses nowadays adopt a 'quality culture' in the belief that it is less expensive to incur internal costs of quality than it is to incur the external costs associated with a poor product.
- TQM sets out to establish a **quality culture** in an organisation, by guaranteeing the quality of work of all staff in all areas of the organisation.
- It is associated with the philosophy of aiming to 'get it right first time', and to 'get it more right next time'. The belief is that the costs of getting the job done properly in the first place will be lower than the costs associated with selling poor-quality products.

ISO 9000

- The **International Standards Organisation** (ISO) 9000 series qualification is a certification of quality management. Firms are required to **document** their procedures in a quality manual, with staff following these agreed procedures. One criticism levelled at the ISO 9000 scheme is that it can be possible for an organisation to achieve low-quality standards through devising procedures that are limited in scope.

Benchmarking

- This occurs when firms measure their production or other performance against a 'benchmark' set by others: for example, the productivity performance of the leading firm in the industry. It is an attempt to seek out the **best practice** by comparing – and then improving – the firm's own practice.
- Benchmarking therefore encourages firms to use **external measures** of performance, focusing on external competition rather than using internal measures of performance. It may prove difficult to obtain accurate benchmark information. However, if this can be obtained:
  - realistic targets can be set for the firm
  - managers and staff are made aware of any competitive disadvantage the firm has.

EXAMINER'S TOP TIP
Make a list of those firms that are best known for providing quality goods and services.

EXAMINER'S TOP TIP
Examiners allow you to save time by using well-known abbreviations, such as TQM and JIT, in your answers.

Quick test

1. *Explain the term 'Kaizen'.*
2. *Give one reason why quality issues are important to any business.*
3. *What is the difference between quality control and quality assurance?*
4. *Explain the term 'competitive advantage'.*
5. *What does 'benchmarking' do?*

1. 'continuous improvement' through encouraging staff to consider how their work can keep being improved   2. e.g. They influence the business's survival and profit.   3. control: checking current quality, e.g. through inspection, of output; assurance: satisfying the customer through setting and implementing agreed quality standards throughout the firm   4. an advantage a firm has over others, e.g. through better quality products   5. It compares the performance of the firm against some external measure, e.g. competitor performance.

Exam-style questions Use the questions to test your progress. Check your answers on pages 92–95.

Exam-style questions

Operations management

1 If large-scale operations are so advantageous, how do small firms continue to survive? Support your answer with appropriate real-life examples. [4]

....

....

....

2 Kneller Ltd makes a component that goes in a popular washing machine. The company has the capacity to make 400 parts a week, and is at present nearly reaching this capacity. The variable cost of each part is £5.00, and the company sells it to the washing machine manufacturer for £10.00. Kneller Ltd's fixed costs average £2 000 per week.

   a Calculate the effect on Kneller's profit if its capacity utilisation fell to:
      i   60% [3]
      ii 75%. [3]

....

....

   Kneller Ltd has received a request from another washing machine manufacturer to supply the component. To do so, Kneller Ltd will have to work flat out, at full capacity.

   b Outline the likely positive and negative effects on Kneller Ltd if it has to work at full capacity for a substantial length of time. [6]

....

....

3 Nice-cream Ltd makes ice cream and other 'sweet treats' for people who cannot eat sugar. The company makes its products using an artificial sweetener. Nice-cream Ltd has a large national market for one of its product lines, which it sells through a national food retailer. The company also offers to make decorative and highly intricate 'Special ice creams for special occasions' such as weddings, for customers who approach the Marketing Department directly.

   a Identify the likely production methods for:
      i   the product lines sold in the national food retailer's shops [1]
      ii   'Special ice creams for special occasions'. [1]

....

....

   b Explain how the differences between the two production methods identified above are likely to affect the work of the production staff at Nice-cream Ltd. [6]

....

....

....

....

4   Holdit Ltd is a small manufacturing company that makes parts used in the computer industry. One item it uses costs £10 from a supplier. Holdit Ltd's ordering cost is £40 per order, and the company calculates its holding cost as £3 per unit of stock.

   a) Calculate the Economic Order Quantity (EOQ) for this stock item. [2]

   ....

   b) Outline why it is important for Holdit Ltd to calculate the EOQ. [3]

   ....

   ....

5   Tins & Bins Ltd manufactures tins and other containers used by the food-processing industry. This is a highly competitive market, so the managers of Tins & Bins Ltd are aware of the importance of controlling costs.
    In recent months, the Production Manager has noticed a build-up of stocks in the stores and also on the factory floor. According to his calculations, there was enough stock to keep production going for nearly three months. He was also concerned when he found some stocks of materials that were no longer being used in the production process. The Production Manager is therefore thinking of introducing a just-in-time system.

   a) Explain how **two** costs, met by Tins & Bins Ltd as a result of holding these stocks, are higher than necessary. [4]

   ....

   ....

   ....

   b) Suggest **one** major problem that the introduction of a just-in-time system is likely to create for Tins & Bins Ltd. [3]

   ....

   ....

6   Teach & Train Ltd is a private-sector training agency, offering work-related courses for young people. It has close links with Makkem Ltd, a local manufacturing company, and trains Makkem Ltd's apprentices. Both these businesses have recently adopted the 'Total Quality Management' philosophy.

   Outline how implementing TQM is likely to affect the work of staff in both companies. [8]

   ....

   ....

   ....

   ....

   ....

   ....

   ....

                                                                           Total: /44

External influences (pp. 4–17)

1 Demand and supply movements can be predicted. For example, the builder could assess the likely changing demand for different types of dwellings, e.g. detached homes, one-bedroomed flats. The builder might also be able to predict the likely responses of competitors.

The builder may consider moving into new markets as a result of expected changes, e.g. seeking building contracts in different parts of the UK where the demand for new homes is expected to increase. By trying to anticipate changes in demand and supply, the builder can therefore anticipate price movements, and budget accordingly.

2 a Monetary policy is associated with the use of interest rates to control the level of demand in an economy such as the UK's. Fiscal policy also helps control demand, but through the use of taxation measures and government spending.

b The UK Government is no longer fully in control of monetary (and therefore interest-rate) policy. It cannot, therefore, rely on monetary policy alone to control inflation. It is in control of the fiscal policy, and can use this policy selectively in order to reduce the income of certain households of groups of people (e.g. smokers).

3 Increasing demand is good in that it encourages firms to invest, and therefore buy new equipment and take on additional staff – which, in turn, increases individuals' wealth and other firms' profits. Increasing demand is bad where it leads to substantial inflation, which can, in turn, encourage the growth of imports at the expense of exports, and affect the UK's competitiveness and its balance of trade.

4 The countries to which the exporters are selling can buy more pounds sterling for each dollar. As a result, the UK exporters can cut their prices, making them more competitive in the USA, which should improve their sales.

5 Rising inflation is good in that any loan or other borrowing falls in real value (although there are increased costs of servicing the loan, i.e. higher interest payments). Cost increases can more easily be passed on in the form of higher prices. It is bad in that it becomes more difficult to plan and budget for the future; and employees are more likely to put pressure on firms for higher wages, thereby increasing costs.

6 a Occupational immobility is due to a lack of skill or training to do the vacant job. Geographical immobility is due to the unwillingness of employees to move regions to take up a new job.

b occupational – Unemployed train driver not having computer skills to apply for a job in computer programming.

geographical – Unemployed teacher in the north of England not being prepared to move to the south-east to take up work, because of house prices and other high living costs.

7 If the firms are in a high-cost area of the UK, such as the south-east of England, staff may not be prepared to move there due to high costs (geographical mobility). If the staff need certain skills, the firm may not be able to get these staff because the unemployed do not possess these skills, or may not be prepared to retrain to gain them (occupational mobility).

8 UK and EU law will limit and control UK business: for example, the Sale and Supply of Goods Act 1994 ensures that goods must be of a satisfactory quality, and if sold by description they must fit that description. UK and EU law also provides a framework within which business operates: for example, the Health and Safety at Work Act 1974 sets the legal framework that allows a business to plan how work will be carried out on its premises.

9 Forms of discrimination found include: sex discrimination (e.g. there is evidence that in many occupations women are still paid less than men for doing the same work); racial discrimination (e.g. there is evidence that some minority ethnic (black and Asian British) staff are discriminated against for recruitment or promotion); disability discrimination (e.g. employers not taking the needs – such as mobility and access – of disabled staff into account). The UK has passed a range of Acts (Sex Discrimination, Race Relations, Disability Discrimination) to provide legal protection for those being discriminated against.

10 Consumer direct action, e.g. avoiding certain products sold (such as those imported from certain countries, or containing certain ingredients), affects the buying policy of Sainsburys and Asda. The fact of consumers wishing to buy environmentally friendly products also influences sources of supply, product positioning in the store, and marketing policy. Increased consumer interest in recycling affects the choice of packaging for Sainsbury and Asda 'own product' items.

Objectives and strategy (pp. 18–25)

1 a Surprise Fries to supply, and Natalie to use, all fixtures and fittings; Natalie to pay Surprise Fries a percentage of her takings (or profits)

b advantages: Natalie gains a recognised product, backed up by marketing and other business support, and receives business advice (she would not receive this if she operated as a sole trader). disadvantages: Natalie is tied to supplying Surprise Fries products, and she has to pay a certain percentage of her profits to this franchisor.

c Expansion is possible without having to make a large investment. Natalie will be highly motivated to sell Surprise Fries products to make a profit for herself.

2 a short-term: to survive in business for the first year; to at least break even in the first year;

long-term: to make sufficient profit to be at least as well off as when being employed

b to become the first choice for local people who wish to buy garden and other wooden items, by providing them with high-quality, durable and value-for-money products

3 Social: changing trends in clothes affects products sold, ageing population affects how clothes for different age ranges are promoted and displayed;

Technological: advances in scanning and other store-based technology means staff training must take place, improvements in handling and storing products makes distribution more efficient;

Economic: changes in interest rates affects demand for clothes, if the economy is in recession, demand for certain types of clothes may fall, meaning the pricing policy of such clothes needs reviewing;

Political: a decision to join the 'Eurozone' will make it easier for the company to buy clothes from, or sell clothes to, the rest of the EU, new health and safety laws may mean store layout needs changing

4 There will be no change in the incorporated status of Mercante Ltd. However, the directors will need to consider the effect of any growth in the company as a result of additional capital becoming available: e.g. the likelihood of economies of scale, or the increase in the company's market share. Larger size may also bring drawbacks, e.g. diseconomies of scale. The directors will also have to disclose more financial and other information about the company and, since it is now quoted on The Stock Exchange, they will need to consider the threat of a possible takeover.

Marketing (pp. 26–45)

1 advantages: As a small company, TieBuy Ltd should be able to adapt quickly to changing market conditions in its segment. By concentrating on a single product it may be able to create a particular and unique image.
disadvantages: There is no diversification so TieBuy Ltd relies on consumer demand for ties remaining constant. As a small company it cannot gain from economies of scale and may not be price-competitive compared with larger businesses making ties.

2 (For each product, alternative bases for segmentation would be acceptable.)
  a geodemographic – to locate near a suitable residential or work area
  b demographic – to identify the socio-economic class of students
  c behavioural – to analyse customer brand-loyalty.

3 primary research: design a questionnaire to interview (face to face) all users of the restaurant, and all hotel guests, undertake a postal survey of (an area of) the local town to assess possible interest, research into the potential competition (i.e. the local gymnasia and health clubs in the town) by checking membership, prices, etc.; secondary research: check government statistics (e.g. *Social Trends*) and other information to discover any trends associated with health and exercise

4 a The range of products sold by Hughes Ltd.
  b BranBiscuit: 'growth' because it is recently introduced and sales are growing;
  Chunky Chews: 'maturity' because it is the market leader and a high seller;
  Dunk'em Delights: 'decline' since sales are falling;
  Fruitee Fig Bars: 'introduction' since it has just been launched;
  Minty Munchies: 'maturity' because sales have returned to their peak figures
  c Evaluate the proposal to make a new cereal bar to see if the product is feasible, check whether there is a gap in the market for such a bar, and assess any limitations such as availability of ingredients. Having made a decision to accept the new proposal, check resources needed and then obtain them so that a prototype bar can be developed to check its likely market appeal, price and cost. The bar is then test marketed, e.g. in one area of the UK, to obtain customer feedback so any necessary modifications can be made. Finally, launch the new cereal bar onto the UK market, and evaluate its success by assessing consumer reaction.
  d Minty Munchies: It has been renamed and has redesigned packaging.
  e The traditional channel of producer–wholesaler–retailer– consumer seems the most appropriate because the biscuits and cereal bars are not sold through large retailers. The traditional channel means that the wholesalers will take Hughes Ltd's biscuits, store and promote them for the company, and give the company market intelligence information. This channel is also suitable for the retailers since these are small and independent and, as a result, will need the wholesaler's service of breaking bulk.
  f a penetration strategy: The company is not the market leader, and needs to gain a foothold in the market. A penetration strategy is low-price, which will mean the cereal bar is competitively priced, and this should encourage initial sales of the bar.

5 a local paper: A number of local people will be interested in the car, and would expect to see second-hand cars advertised here (a section is normally devoted to these adverts). It is a relatively cheap source for a private seller.
  b national TV: Many people watching the TV will have seen the film, and many of these will have the games console, so – even though the advert is expensive – a mass market is being targeted. The sound and movement of the game can be shown in the advert, to persuade people to buy.
  c local radio: People in the locality of the centre and radio station will be the ones who are interested in the new store. Radio is not very expensive, and it can reach a wide audience.

6 a 10% / 5% = 2.0.
  b Price-elastic.
  c The managers seem to be justified: the previous weekly revenue was £10 × 10 000 = £100 000, whereas the new weekly revenue is £9.50 × 11 000 = £104 500, and increased revenue of £4 500. However, we do not know the profit margin on the product, so cannot calculate the effect on overall profits.

Finance and accounting (pp. 46–61)

1 Direct costs are those that can be directly linked to making the product. Indirect costs, also known as overheads, are not directly linked. Examples of direct costs for Merchant Ltd will be the raw materials from which its CDs and DVDs are made, and the wages of the staff actually pressing and making these products. Examples of its indirect costs are any business rent and rates it pays, interest charges on any loans it has, depreciation on fixed assets such as vehicles used to deliver its products, and administrative expenses associated with its CDs and DVDs.

2

Output (units)	Fixed costs	Variable costs	Total costs	Average total costs
	£	£	£	£
1 000	200 000	15 000	215 000	215.00
2 000	200 000	30 000	230 000	115.00
3 000	200 000	45 000	245 000	81.67
4 000	200 000	60 000	260 000	65.00

The average total costs are falling as the output increases. The reason for this is that the £200 000 fixed costs are being divided amongst higher output figures, giving a lower average fixed cost per unit of output.

3 Break-even analysis can be used to explore changes in selling price. The effect of, for example, a fall in selling price on the firm's break-even point might be calculated and discussed. In this case, however, there is evidence that the company sells more than one product, so if the sales 'mix' (proportion of different products being sold) changes, then break-even analysis becomes difficult to use. Furthermore, the company is selling in both home and overseas markets, so it may use a range of different pricing strategies for these different markets. If it does so, break-even analysis is again difficult to use.

4 **a)** £5.00 – (£1.25 + £0.50 + £0.25) = £3.00.
   b) Output: £150 000/£3.00 = 50 000. Revenue: 50 000 x £5.00 = £250 000.
   c) Margin of safety: 75 000 – 50 000 = 25 000 T-shirts.

5 Some debtors may not pay on time; some creditors may decide to reduce the credit payment periods allowed to the business. The business may implement tighter credit control, or offer discounts for prompt payments to its debtors to improve cash inflow; it may renegotiate its credit terms with suppliers, or only use those suppliers who offer better credit terms.

6 **a** A bank overdraft is an appropriate source to buy materials and pay staff. This is short term and flexible so payments can be made as and when required. To buy the machine a bank loan would be appropriate. The digger needs to be bought, and is costly, so partners can take out a loan for the full cost, and then budget for interest payments and repayment of the loan.
   b advantages: There is no large outlay of cash required. The digger need only be leased for the duration of the project. disadvantages: The partners are paying for something they will never own. They will have to lease another digger for future projects.

7 **a** sales; production; cash
   b The sales budget identifies the volume of sales expected. This figure helps the firm calculate how many to make (production budget). Cash in (from sales) and out (to pay for material and labour used in production) will feature in the cash budget.
   c The key functions are co-ordinated – for example, the sales and production departments will co-operate to a greater extent because their budgets need to be co-ordinated. Staff will be motivated – for example, sales and production staff will be set targets to achieve, and the Finance Department staff will want to ensure that actual cash flow is similar to that in the cash budget.

8

	Budget (£)	Actual (£)	Variances (£)
Sales	675 000	750 000	75 000 Fav
Materials	155 000	165 000	10 000 Adv
Labour	200 000	190 000	10 000 Fav
Overheads	70 000	75 000	5 000 Adv
Profit	250 000	320 000	70 000 Fav

Sales: more units sold; materials: higher unit cost; labour: cheaper grade used; overheads: business rates more expensive than expected.

People in organisations (pp. 62–77)

1 **a** The organisation chart shows the relatively narrow span of control, with up to five levels in the hierarchy. This suggests the company's lines of communication are likely to be formal and its decision-making may be slow, especially as it operates in several locations.
   b TootyFrooty Ltd could be reorganised to become matrix-based, basing its structure either on each product or each factory. This could result in more motivated staff, and overcome the co-ordination and other problems being faced by the Production Manager.

2 **a)** Tasks on the assembly line are likely to be repetitive, and therefore boring. Evidence shows that pay is not necessarily the main motivator, as suggested by Herzberg. Staff may feel they cannot achieve their full potential (Maslow's self-actualisation), and managers may pay them little attention (Mayo's Hawthorne Effect). The working conditions – Herzberg's hygiene factors – are poor, which can cause low morale and motivation.
   b) The company could consider implementing a job-rotation scheme, whereby individuals move between different jobs. A job-enrichment scheme could be introduced, although the staff might need to be trained in new skills so they could carry out the greater range of tasks associated with job enrichment. Improved working conditions will help avoid negative motivation.

3 **a)** autocratic management: The manager makes all major decisions without consulting staff. The emphasis is on individual decision-taking rather than group decision-making.
   b) Where staff are poorly trained and lack the necessary skills and/or knowledge to make decisions themselves – perhaps when a new product has been launched.
   c) Even though profit targets have been exceeded, Irene seems to lack staff support (high labour turnover), and a teamwork approach may reduce labour turnover, and also help staff understand the new product. As a result, motivation should improve and skills should be developed.
   d) A democratic style may be appropriate because staff will become more involved in decision-making, and therefore more motivated. Communication would become more two-way, with the staff being able to make suggestions concerning the new product. However, this style would have to be introduced gradually since the staff may only be used to a more autocratic approach and not be willing to participate to such a great extent.

4 **a)** Staff motivation fell through boredom (repetitive tasks all day), with no incentive to work hard/sell insurance.
   b) introduction of an incentive-based payment scheme: Staff are now encouraged to sell insurance, since the more sold, the higher the wage. As a result, sales were increased.
   c) Unrealistic targets may be set; staff may be finding it impossible to sell enough policies to earn as much as they did when receiving a fixed wage.
   d) job rotation: limited opportunities since virtually all the work in the call centre is the same;
   job enrichment: again limited scope since there does not appear to be the opportunity for staff to develop a range of skills or to work as a team, although teams might be set up and team bonuses offered in an attempt to improve motivation and attendance

5 The insurance company will attempt to overcome this problem in both the short and longer term by producing a new – or revising its existing – workforce plan. The plan will need to be based on the company's goals and objectives, and will examine how best to improve the skills of existing staff, and how to recruit new staff with suitable skills. The company's plan will need to take into account current and future trends in the labour market – relevant ones for this firm may be the increase in part-time and flexible working, and the increasing number of women seeking work.

6 job descriptions: The food retailer will need to identify exactly what the person is to do – e.g. for warehouse staff, details of paperwork to be checked, loads to be handled, hours of work, location, training in handling bulky objects, to whom responsible. This ensures staff know their duties and responsibilities, which is important in a large organisation with different departments.

person specifications: The retailer will need to select suitable people so that efficiency is at least maintained, and customers are kept happy – for example, checkout operator: ability to handle money, pleasant personality, responsible attitude, able to use checkout machinery, aware of food-related hygiene issues, can work as part of a team

Operations management (pp. 78–91)

1 Large-scale production brings many advantages to a firm. Examples include bulk-buying economies (e.g. retailers such as Tesco and BHS being able to buy clothing in bulk and therefore at relatively cheap prices), and financial economies (e.g. car manufacturers such as Ford and Vauxhall being able to obtain large amounts of capital and loans).
Small firms tend to survive for three main reasons. First, they may have a local demand for their products: examples include 'high-street' independent hairdressers and newsagents. Second, it may be the wish of the owner(s) to keep the size of the firm small: one reason is that power and control will not be lost by the owners. Third, being small can bring a number of strengths to a firm, including flexibility (e.g. the hairdresser can quickly change advertising, and offer different hair-styles as soon as fashions change), and efficient communication (e.g. the newsagent can easily contact other staff, and delivery boys and girls).

2 a) i) Sales are (60% × 400) × £15 = £3 600.
Variable costs are (60% × 400) × £7 = £1 680; fixed costs are £2 000; total costs are £3 680. Weekly loss is therefore £80.

ii) Sales are (75% × 400) × £15 = £4 500.
Variable costs are (75% × 400) × £7 = £2 100; fixed costs are £2 000; total costs are £4 100. Weekly profit is therefore £400.

b) Profits will increase because fixed costs are being spread over a greater output (unit fixed costs would be £2 000/400 = £5, the lowest possible figure). However, resources will be stretched: managers and other staff will be put under additional pressure, which may affect attendance and morale generally; it may not be possible to maintain the machinery as efficiently, resulting in breakdowns; if this happens, it will affect the ability of Kneller Ltd to meet the orders of both its existing and its new customer. As a result, the company may lose its contracts.

3 a) i) flow production (a large national market);
ii) job production.

b) Flow production of the nationally available ice cream means that the company will have invested heavily in capital equipment such as machines for making ice cream. Staff who work on these machines are not likely to be highly skilled, unlike those staff who make the decorative and intricate special ice creams. The production staff operating the flow-line machinery may find themselves bored if the tasks are repetitive, which they are likely to be. As a result, absenteeism levels are probably higher when compared with the staff working

on the special products. Morale amongst flow-line staff is also likely to be lower, since the staff working on the special ice creams can utilise a much wider range of skills.

4 a) $\text{EOQ} = \sqrt{\dfrac{2 \times 40 \times 2000}{3}}$ = 230 (or 231) units.

b) As a result of calculating the EOQ, Holdit Ltd can balance the cost of placing an order with the cost of holding stock, and keep its overall stockholding costs to a minimum.

5 a) There will be stockholding costs linked to the stores space the excess stock is taking up. First, more Stores staff than necessary may be being employed, which increases labour costs related to stock. Second, stock 'ties up' cash, which would be free for Tins & Bins Ltd to use elsewhere: this is an opportunity cost of excessive stock.

b) Tins & Bins Ltd faces the problem of finding reliable suppliers of the tin and other materials it needs. These suppliers must not only be able to meet tight delivery deadlines: they must also deliver a quality product free from defects, otherwise production at Tins & Bins Ltd may come to a halt, losing sales in its competitive market-place.

6 Both companies will adopt the 'get it right first time; get it more right next time' philosophy of TQM. This will result in all employees becoming involved in this quality framework, requiring them to ensure that – at all stages of production in Makkem Ltd, and all training stages in Teach & Train Ltd – quality is achieved and at least maintained. In both businesses the needs of the clients – external and internal – will be fully considered: for example, Teach & Train Ltd will consider the needs of Makkem Ltd's employees. The acceptance of internal colleagues as clients will help to develop teamwork in each company. All employees will work together, with the shared goal of improving the quality of their output.

Index